From A Broken Place

From A Broken Place

Danielle Singleton

Flourish Publishing
Ladson, SC

From A Broken Place
Published by:
Flourish Publishing
Ladson, South Carolina
Flourishingher39@gmail.com
Danielle Singleton, Publisher
Quality Press.info, Book Packager

DEDICATION

With hands lifted I give all the glory, honor, and praise to the Almighty, True, and Living God! The biggest Thank you for loving and choosing me to carry out an assignment of such a magnitude as this. Thank you for never leaving my side. It was You who carried me through every storm, and I'm so glad that I came to the knowledge that You were "there all the time." Thank you for saving me, filling me with Your Holy Spirit, and placing Your precious gifts on the inside of me. You made me worthy and I will love and praise You for the rest of my days! Thank You because I began this journey *Broken*, and through it, you have restored me and made me Whole. I Love You Lord!

WITH LOVE AND ACKNOWLEDGEMENT

Emmanuel, Thank you for your unfailing, intentional, unconditional, unwavering, consistent, Love! It was your love that has healed me in places I never knew I needed to be healed. Thank you for the constant encouragement and push that I needed to be able to write this book and to do many other things in life. Your "I'm Proud of You's, You Can Do This's, and I Got Your Back's" kept me going at many points when I wanted to give up. Thank you for always wiping my tears and calming my fears. You were made for me, and I COULDN'T have done this the way I've done this, without you! It's been a pleasure being your wife for these last 20 years, and it will continue to be a pleasure for the rest of our lives. I love you Always, Forever, Infinity, to Eternity.

To My "Great 8" - Saniyah, Emmanuel Jr, Jeremiah, Josiah, Ayanah, Micah, Isaiah, and Alaiyah…each of you was a gift from God to me (including your sibling in Heaven). If you didn't know, the Lord spoke and said he would use my womb to birth out a line of Prophets which he would use for His Glory. God has a purpose for each of your individual lives, but God also brought you here to save me. You all were the reason

I never gave up; you were the reason I've survived! You were the reason I became a Generational Curse Breaker (GCB). Each of you was assigned to me to love, nurture, and care for and I pray that I have and will continue to fulfill my assignment as your Mama for the rest of my days. I pray the Lord's face continues to shine upon each of you and that salvation and God's goodness continue to be your portion, Thank You for loving me and encouraging me to write this book! I Love each one of you Always, Forever, Infinity, to Eternity

To My Uncle Duane Moore Sr. and My Granny(in-law) …. Uncle, the role you played in my life may have been counted as minor, but in the eyes of the Lord and in my heart it was major. Thank you for all your loving embraces and for the care of my soul. 10 minutes of you ministering to me kickstarted my journey with Christ and I've been doing my best to live for God ever since. You will always be a part of my testimony! Pastor E. Snell, (granny) thank you for making sure I received the gift of the Holy Spirit, for believing in Emmanuel and I, and joining us in Holy Matrimony! A lot of people didn't believe we were ready, but you heard the voice of God and followed his instruction. Thank you for being a vessel used to help establish my walk with God and thank you for your prayers that we are still living off of today. Your life living was an example and a testimony to the goodness of the Lord! Continue to Rest safely in the arms of the Lord, until we meet again and rejoice together on streets of Gold. I love you both.

To My Aunt Alice Fordham, My Grandmama (in law), Mrs. Rebecca Green, and My Grandfather Mauriello Lea, thank you for gently loving and caring for me and filling voids that you had no idea that you were filling. Each of you gave me love in a pure form and because of that, I knew that I wasn't unlovable and that God had sent each of you to walk beside me and hold my hand in those times when I needed someone the most. I wish that you were here to see me healed and whole and to know that your kindness and love contributed to the woman I am today, but it does my heart gladness to know that all of you are resting in the arms of the Lord and cheering me on from a heavenly place. I LOVE YOU and miss you all. Continue to Sleep In Peace. Until we meet again.

X

CONTENTS

CHAPTER 1

THE FAMILY TREE

Hey Y'all! My name is Danielle, but everyone calls me Dani…Dani with an "I." For as long as I can remember, I've always been this quiet-natured, shy girl, with a lot of questions! I grew up in South Carolina with my maternal grandparents, my mother, and my two aunts. My mom was very young when she gave birth to me. So young, I'm told, I mistook her for my sister and my grandparents for my parents. I had to be taught to call her "Mama" instead of Denise.

This meant I had a "mama," a "mommy," a "daddy," and my two aunts, Nikki and Paris. I vaguely remember the times when my mother lived in the house on Crocker Ave with me. She had given birth to me at age 14, three days short of her 15th Birthday, and by the time I was two years old, she had moved out completely and given birth to my brother. I stayed at the house on Crocker Ave with my grandparents until we moved to Mason Street, just before I started school. During this period, I remember my mother 'coming and going.'

As children, we weren't allowed to sit on my grandmother's furniture, so when my mom would come through the door to visit, I'd either be sitting on the living room floor or the orange & brown linoleum floor in our bedroom. She'd walk in and say, "Hi Dani," to which I'd always reply, "Hi" or "Hi Mama." She'd look at me long and hard as she walked by. I didn't know it then, but she'd quickly look me over to see if I resembled her terrible childhood. Years later, as she told me this, my mind couldn't help but wonder if she had seen what she was looking for, would it have been enough to make her take me with her? After greeting me and looking me over, she'd disappear for a brief time with "Mommy" (my grandmother) and I'd hear them laughing and talking, and then she'd leave the way she came. "Bye Dani" ... "Bye Mama" ... another long stare, and she was gone.

Two questions troubled me from a very young age.... Number 1, "Why doesn't she ever talk to me or take me with her?" ... and Number 2, "She's such a pretty lady, but why doesn't she look like anyone at our house?" It would take years until I'd find out the answers to most of my questions. My aunties were good to me during my childhood, besides the fact that my Aunt Nikki got upset when she'd have to give me her Barbie Doll accessories. Lol. She was the next oldest after my mom, and then my Aunt Paris, making her the baby of the bunch. I loved them both. Auntie Nikki was book-smart, and a bit of a hothead. She was a real 'No Nonsense' kind of girl. She wasn't afraid to fight; in fact, I heard she busted many girls up back in the day, lol. She was the one who told me to be fearless. "It doesn't matter who they are or how big they are, you always stand up for yourself. The bigger they are, the harder they fall. Hit 'em with the left first and finish 'em with the right!" You couldn't tell me I wasn't a professional boxer with that advice (lol).

My other auntie, Paris, was the fun one. She was 11 years older than me, and she was the one who taught me how to dance… whatever dance moves were out, the Cabbage Patch, the Running Man, the MC Hammer, you name it! Even years later after she moved out, she'd come back to visit and we'd do the Butterfly, the KidNPlay, the (TLC) Creep, etc., lol. She also loved to laugh, and her smile brightened up any room. Even to this day, she always laughs at my jokes, lol. My grandfather was the sole provider for the family, so I only saw him in the evenings. When he'd come home from work, he and my grandmother would drink beer and smoke cigarettes. Even though my mother wasn't present, life was ok, but life for me would change, quickly! It would lead me on a roller coaster of emotional trauma. I'd fight hard to get off that roller coaster ride, but every time I'd think I was off; the seatbelt would violently snatch me back into its raggedy seat and the ride would start all over again! I'd find out some hard truths, learn some painful lessons, walk alone, and eventually meet God who would carry me through it all.

By the time I was five years old and ready to start Kindergarten, my mom had given birth to three more children, all boys! I was excited to be a big sister to my brothers. I hoped that one day we'd have a strong bond, even though we grew up in separate homes. I'd be their protector and they'd be mine. My mom would come to get me, and I'd spend the weekends with them from time to time, and now and then they'd come over to my house. Tears burned my eyes when it was time for them to leave. I didn't have any idea why they didn't come over much or why my mom still didn't want me to live with them. All I know is that I formed the bond I wanted with my real brothers, with my cousin Jack.

Finally, the time for me to start school had come! It was both exciting and terrifying. We had a sheltered life on Mason Street. Not a lot of people visited, and we didn't get to go to a lot of places. Most of my days were spent sitting Indian-style on that orange & brown linoleum floor. I hated that floor! It had little orange and brown hexagon shapes all over it. It was cold and because we'd sit there for so many hours, my legs would ache and stick to it. I would think about my mom often and see how many times it took me to rub my finger around and around those hexagons until she returned for another visit. Of course, I always lost count, but it was fun to tell myself that by the time I counted to 100 times around the shape she would be back, and the next time she might take me with her for good. That never came true though, so going to school became a pleasant escape for me. I loved school! The smell of it, the colors, the shapes, the people, the classrooms, and my teachers; my favorite teacher was my second-grade teacher Ms. J. I wasn't even afraid that all our kindergarten classrooms were in the basement of the school. You could say I was a bit shy and timid though. I wasn't sure how to interact with people because we weren't used to being around anyone besides my grandparents, and there was no conversational communication between adults and children at home. Now that I think of it, even Jackson and I didn't talk to each other much unless we snuck and did it. Noise wasn't tolerated, and talking was considered noise. He and I developed a 'whisper and eye contact' form of communication.

Jackson was my Aunt Paris's son and somehow, he had gotten left behind at my grandparents' house as well. Like my mom, my aunt was also young when she had him. There were rumors about who his father was, but we never actually found out the truth. Something had changed on Mason Street after my aunts moved out. It seems like my grandparents became increasingly short-tempered and MEAN, especially my grandmother. School was the escape I needed. I found no faults with school, except one thing…. NAPTIME. I didn't like it at all. *I mean, help me understand why I needed to lie down when I was not tired!* Storytime made up for it though. I was amazed and intrigued by storytelling, books, reading and writing. "If You Give a Mouse A Cookie," was my favorite book! Dr Seuss's "The Grinch" gave me the creeps, but "Sam I Am" was my absolute favorite story! I think it had something to do with the fact that we got to make green eggs and ham in class, which was delicious, by the way!

My kindergarten class experience went great. That all changed in a weird way when a new girl transferred to our school and was put in our class. Her name was Reese, and we quickly became friends. We did everything together! We stood in line, we played at recess, we ate lunch, we went to the bathroom, tied each other's shoes, played in each other's hair, and napped together! She was my best friend, and then one day it all changed. Naptime was after recess with snack time and dismissal directly after. At recess one day, I told Reese how much I hated taking naps. We proceeded to go inside and set up our kinder mats, mine on the red side, hers on the blue. We laid down and spread out our cover that we shared like we did every other day. Something about this time was different though. She scooted over and whispered, "I know how to help you go to sleep." I answered back, "How?" I was not prepared for what happened next... I felt her hand cross over to my side of the mat and before I knew it, this girl quickly put her hand down my pants. I was in disbelief and shock! I didn't know what to do or say. I didn't understand what was happening. In my mind, I was saying STOP IT! But the words would not come up my throat and leave my lips! She never did anything to the nature of penetration, but she just laid her hand in "my area of privacy" and then took her hand out. She explained that I should do this to myself, and she tried to demonstrate a massaging motion. She said this helped her fall asleep at night.

No one had ever discussed what to do if someone ever touched my private parts. No one had ever said that they were off limits and that I should tell someone if I was touched inappropriately or made to feel uncomfortable, so I didn't know what to do. All I knew was that it made me feel dirty and it felt wrong and…. familiar. I didn't like feeling like this. We got up from naptime and everyone was ready for a snack. I wasn't hungry after what had just happened. I quietly asked Ms. Sharp if I could take my CHEEZ-ITZ home instead. From then on, instead of sleeping on my back and sharing a cover, I slept on my side with my back toward Reese and I let her keep the cover! My friend and I never spoke of the incident, but I couldn't help but feel broken and sad because I could no longer be friends with the friend I had grown to love and cherish. At 5 years old, I lost trust in one of the closest relationships I had. I wanted to talk to my mom about it but the lack of communication between her and me made it hard for me to come out and say what happened to me that day. I would never tell anyone what happened until I got married and confided in my husband about it. He made a valid point which was Reese didn't really understand what she was doing and that just maybe she had been violated too. It never dawned on me to think about it that way until he said it.

Reese ended up leaving my school and I wouldn't see her again for another 25+ years. I tucked the violation away in my mind and went on with life like it never happened, but every so often things would trigger it in my memory. The guilt and shame of it would trigger often as well. I felt like what had happened was my fault for not stopping it. I became disgusted with myself at 5 years old… Despite that incident, Kindergarten Year went on and I excelled. Weeks passed after Reese left and I found myself becoming a normal 5-year-old. It was time to do our "Family Tree" project. All the kids at my table had these large extended trees with aunts, uncles, grandparents, parents, siblings, cousins, and even godparents, but my tree was so small with just a few branches. One of my classmates leaned over and asked, "Why do you have 2 moms and one Dad?" I explained to him that one was my real mom, and one was my grandmother, and where it said "Dad" was my grandfather. He paused and said, "Oh that's cool, but umm…where is your dad?' At this point, I'm confused because I didn't know what he meant. My grandfather was my dad. My brothers had a dad, and my cousins had a dad, but me and Jack didn't. Our mothers had had us by themselves.

He looked at me like I was crazy. "No, my big cousin said that everyone has a mom and a dad. Some Dads just run away from home and never come back." I felt like he was just talking and didn't know what he was talking about, and I wasn't going to ask him anything about no dads! I mean there is no way I had a dad and BOTH he and my mother had left me…there's just no way…right? Just then I looked at his drawing and saw that he had drawn roots into the ground with names on them. "Who are they?" I asked. "My family members who died," he said as he continued coloring. I started to realize that My tree lacked so much. Not many branches, and no roots. *How can a tree grow without roots? Why don't I know anybody besides the people that live in my house? Do I have a dad? If so, where is he?* All these questions, and I decided to keep them to myself. I didn't want to get in trouble with my grandma. She didn't like it when we asked questions. That was being disrespectful and "grown." Children were not supposed to question adults. All of this was a lot to shoulder at 5 and 6 years old.

PAUSE:

Parents, please be mindful of who your children are engaging with. Ask them how their day was at school and allow them to tell you every detail of their day. Even when you don't necessarily want to hear it. You don't know what they will expose when they feel comfortable enough to talk to you and feel like you care. Just because your child is not exposed to certain things in your home and your presence doesn't mean they can't be exposed to it through another child or adult. Teach them at an early age that no one is allowed to touch them in their areas of privacy nor make them uncomfortable through speech or touch. No one in my world protected me in that area of my life and at 19 years old.... I found out exactly why...

CHAPTER 2

MASON STREET

Growing up on Mason Street was different. It was almost like a prison. As children, we may not have fully understood that we were in bondage, but I always sensed that there was this whole other world that we didn't have access to. Again, this was because our parents had chosen to leave us there. Nevertheless, I was happy I didn't have to be there alone. My cousin Jackson, we called him Jack, was living there also. Jack was my Auntie Paris's oldest son. I overheard my grandma on the phone one day saying that my auntie was out living recklessly and "messing around with drugs." Jackson was about 3 years younger than me. I was born in 1985 and he was born in 1988. He was like a brother to me. More like a brother than my real brothers. Our days before becoming school-age were spent mostly sitting Indian-style on the floor watching cartoons. He and I shared a bed for a while. One to the top of the bed and one to the bottom of the bed. It was a twin bed, and we were expected to lay as straight as possible so we would not kick each other or invade each other's space. Because the bed had that noisy plastic on it, when we'd try to reposition ourselves, it would alert my grandparents in the next room. Either one of them would come in fussing at any given moment and there were plenty of times we got popped or slammed back into place. I never understood why they were so angry at us for moving positions while sleeping. "Y'all better keep y'all little *** still!" SLAM. Whatever position you were put in was the one you had better stay in. To this day, my husband jokes that I sleep crazy sometimes, and I tell him that's my way of making up for the times I had to sleep like a mummy. Lol.

Our house had an unusual floor plan before it was remodeled. Through the front door was a wall that held a heater that stretched the entire height of it, a small foyer that opened to the right and left. To the right was a door that led into my grandparents' room, and to the left was the living room, kitchen, a back porch, and a backyard. Which leads you to wonder where the rest of the house was, right? Inside my grandparents' room were two doors. One was the door that led to our room. It was one of those old doors with the old-timey keyholes. The other door was to the door to their walk-thru closet. This closet also led to our room. So, it was like we were inside a secret compartment of the house. The closet was narrow and filled with clothes, mostly jackets. The smell of my grandfather's Old Spice cologne on his clothes nearly suffocated me each time I had to walk through it. Sleeves slapped me in the face, cologne choked me, and pitch-black darkness terrified me. Inside our room was the only bathroom in the house. This meant that if you came over and had to use the bathroom, you'd have to lay eyes on us. Sometimes I think my mom didn't even have to use the bathroom, but it was just her way to check on us. There was also one more small room in the house. This room, which we called the dungeon, was just off our room. It was a cold, damp, small space with an arched entryway. No door. Jack and I were petrified of that space. No one occupied the room, so my Aunt Paris used it to store her stuff when she was between places to stay. Bags of clothes, shoes, and all kinds of other "junk" were in there. I remember my grandmother would always spray her stuff down with Lysol when she brought it over.

The walls were made of what my grandfather called cinderblocks. The concrete blocks would "sweat" causing the room to have that damp, cold, moldy feel. At night I'd look over into the black darkness and hear monsters trying to get out and attack me. I hated turning my back on it because I could feel the beast from the room standing behind me making noises. To keep from being afraid I'd pray and ask God to kill the monsters and imagine that my grandparents were still awake. If they were awake, they'd hear the beast and run in to kill it. Kind of like the rattling plastic on the bed, but instead of slamming me, they'd slam the beast! This is just what I told myself so I wouldn't be afraid. I told Jack that if he could feel my foot by him, he'd be protected. I couldn't let the beast get Jack. The whole time we thought the beast lived in the Dungeon but in reality, the monsters we should have been afraid of lived in the other room. Eventually, my grandfather hammered a sheet up to the archway due to the winter cold seeping through the room into ours. Thank God! I didn't have to see them anymore, but I couldn't help but feel their presence at night. I really disliked Saturdays on Mason Street. I guess that was my grandmother's day to sleep in, which meant we would be super hungry. Jack was too scared to get out of bed so I would sneak out of the bed and peek through the keyhole to see if I could see my grandmother's legs on her bed. If I did, we'd be hungry a little bit longer, if I didn't then I'd better hurry back to bed before she unlocked the door and came in with breakfast.

I didn't know what jail was back then, but as I grew up, I began to compare the two. Locks on the door, preventing us from getting out, breakfast and lunch served through them on the weekends, our windows were painted shut, we had pit-bull guard dogs that ran right under my window, padlocks, and chains on both front and back gates, and little to no communication with the outside world. Years later my sister and I would make jokes about our grandmother being the Warden and our grandfather being the C.O. Although at any given time it seemed as if they switched roles. We did get to eat dinner in the kitchen or the Chow Hall like they call it in prison. We had a small yellow table with white legs, with the chairs to match. Dinner time wasn't a social hour, though, and we knew to eat and not play games at the table. One night Jack and I were sitting at the table eating Bologna and Cheese sandwiches and drinking water. Jack accidentally knocked his cup of water over and it spilled all over my sandwich. Jack was terrified, and I knew that he was going to get hit. I switched cups with him and when my grandmother came in, I told her I wasted my water. I had prepared myself to take the beating. Jack was a small and frail, but loving, boy with such sadness in his eyes. I always felt so bad because while I felt like I didn't have anybody, at least I knew I had people out there somewhere. Jack was on his own. My grandparents were all he had, and I hated the way they treated him. I hated the way he was afraid of them. To my surprise, I didn't get hit, but I was forced to eat the sandwich. The way the wet bread felt in my mouth made me gag and to this day, as a grown adult, I can't eat bologna, or a whole sandwich for that matter without feeling like I want to vomit. That night I ate that disgusting "food" while tears streamed down my face and my throat burned. Jack looked at me and mouthed "I'm sorry."

You see, things had changed on Mason Street. My grandmother was from Brooklyn New York, a "tough cookie," with the mouth of a sailor, and one who didn't take "no mess" from anyone, but she seemed sweeter and loving before all her girls had moved out. She also used to hang out and drink beers with my grandfather and her friends on our street. All that had stopped too because she stopped drinking and smoking, but my grandfather had not. He worked a lot, and I must say he was an excellent provider. He wasn't afraid of hard work, and he never complained about having to take care of his family. But he drank like a fish! We would hear them fuss and fight. It sounded like furniture was being thrown around. Friday nights, which were paydays, were the worst. I'd hear things like. "You think you just gonna spend all the money on beer?" and "All you wanna do is get drunk, I'm tired of this s*** Charles!" My grandmother always stood up for herself, she was not afraid of anyone! Once I even heard her say "I'm tired of you, Charles, I'ma pack up all of me and Jack **** and I'm moving back to New York!" Through drunken speech, I heard him beg for her not to go. She'd never say I was going with her, just her and Jack....

One night when I was in 4th grade the scenario changed from me only hearing them to seeing them have somewhat of a physical altercation. I was packing my lunch for school, and I had just pulled out my purple Barbie lunchbox with the matching thermos and placed it on the counter. My grandfather had come home drunk again, I mean he was tight. Speech slurred, eyes red, stumbling into the wall with a brown paper bag with a can of beer inside it, in his hand. She started in on him immediately. "Where is the money, Charlie?" She walked up to him, and he pushed her! She ran at him full speed, slapped the can out of his hand and ripped the pocket right off his green work uniform pants. This woman snatched the money from his pocket and cussed him out like I had never heard! Just when I thought he was going to slap her down, I looked over and saw him collapse onto the chair in tears. "Rockie, why you always gotta take my money from me?" She looked at him and said, "Because if I don't, your drunk a** will drink it all up, and how we gonna pay the bills, Charlie, huh?" She shot me a look once she realized I was still standing there and told me to go to bed and she'd finish my lunch in the morning. I was afraid for Granddaddy Charles. I went to bed thinking about all the times I had been punished and wondered if he was being punished for something too.

Our beatings consisted of slapping, punching, being chopped with wooden sticks, brushes to the knuckles, belts to the palm of our hands, and beatings with extension cords and 'switches" off the tree, to name a few. Being put on punishment was also torture, and overly extensive. It was like jail's solitary confinement. I hated the feeling of the walls closing in on me. To add to the physical, the emotional and psychological abuse damaged us too. My grandmother had this way of making me feel so low whenever she was mad at me. I felt like she thought I was favored by my grandfather so she would treat me differently. It was almost like she was jealous or something. My grandfather used to work at a warehouse for a major grocery store chain in South Carolina called the Piggly Wiggly. Its logo was a white pig outlined in red. He would bring me and Jack home toys from the store often. I would usually get a new Barbie Doll and accessories to match. I loved Barbies, I even had this one that reminded me of my mother. She was a fair-skinned doll with black hair, just like her.

My mother didn't look like anyone in the family. Her pale skin compared to a soft cream color and everyone else was brown-skinned. I was the color of caramel, and so was my grandmother. My aunts and grandfather were like chocolate. I always wondered why she looked different but there was this show called "The Cosby Show" that had a light-skinned mom, a dark-skinned dad, 3 dark-skinned children, and two fair-skinned daughters. The two fair-skinned daughters were the same complexion as my mom and had similar hair texture, as well. I thought they were a real family that let cameras into their home so people all over could watch and laugh. I figured that if they had an assorted family then it must be normal. I was wrong…. that was a TV show….and my family was holding some secrets that would cause me to lose trust in all of them!

My grandfather seemed to love me a lot. He would take me with him on his adventures all over town. Everyone seemed to know and like him. We'd pass people on the corner and they 'd say things like "What Cha say, Charlie?" and he'd reply, "All right all right, slap me five my brother." When we went to the corner store he would buy me candy. Sometimes we'd stop and he would be talking to people for long periods of time. Once, someone he was talking to went to touch my hair. He completely snapped! "Don't you ever touch her hair!" We started walking and I thought to myself, *why can't he touch my hair, I must have magical hair or something.* My grandfather was very superstitious; so, for a stranger to touch your hair, it could possibly fall out or they would take a piece of your hair and use it for witchcraft. He believes in "not splitting a pole, don't put a hat on the bed, if you sweep someone's foot, you have to spit on the broom, don't walk under a ladder, etc." but in this case, I didn't want nobody making my hair fall out or putting witchcraft on me, so I agreed, don't touch my hair, sir, lol.

I took our walks as mini adventures, and even now when I go back to the Mason Street Area, I see buildings and stores I remember passing and touching on our walks. The hood hasn't changed much at all. I will never forget this one time we walked to this house. We didn't do that often. We usually went to stores, banks, places to pay bills, the library, stuff like that. This house was down a side street behind a church called Noah's Ark. It was filled with people… People I'd never seen before. This woman came out and my grandfather went into a back room with her. He left me up in the living room of the house with all these adults who were drinking and smoking. *What house was this? What was he doing? Who are these people? Does my grandmother know?* I don't remember how long we were there; I just remember him holding my hand on the walk back home and asking me not to tell Grandmother where we went. I said OK, and by the time we got home I was so exhausted that I went to bed. I didn't ever question him about the incident, and eventually, I put it out of my mind that it even happened. Besides, I figured I owed him one. When my grandmother would be on my case, for whatever reason, my grandfather would step in and take up for me.

Her response was always something derogatory. "Yea you always taking up for this B****, you want her, here you take her!" She'd shove me in his direction. He would ask her to stop it, but she'd cuss and fuss all the way to her room and SLAM the door. He didn't know whether to console me or not so each time he'd walk off to the room and continue fussing or go to another part of the house. Each time I was left feeling sad, confused, and dirty. The next day, after one of these episodes, she would stop speaking to me. The silent treatment would last sometimes for a week. Every time it would end in me apologizing for something I didn't do. I wanted to be loved and accepted and if an apology was what I had to do, then so be it. I didn't realize it but as a child, I was being manipulated and emotionally abused. Every time I was called a "B****" or "HIS little B****" I was reduced smaller and smaller on the inside until I felt like nothing. The words of her verbal abuse hurt just like a punch to the stomach. I didn't understand this treatment. I was an innocent child who had to deal with the issues and trauma of the adults in my life all while acquiring trauma of my own. *Would someone ever come and get me out of this?* Unfortunately, no one ever came.

On a better note, I believe she favored Jack. It seemed like she loved him more than she loved me. I was ok with that and glad that he wasn't receiving the same treatment, but my grandfather treated him the way my grandmother treated me. Because Jackson was frail and acted feminine, I believe my grandfather thought he could beat it out of him. The beatings didn't toughen him up, it only made Jackson fear him. I hated my grandfather for that. No one seemed to care though, and our mother's visits were now few and far between and we were left forgotten about while the walls of Mason Street slowly closed in on us.

VERBAL ABUSE:
A range of words or behaviors used to manipulate, intimidate, and maintain power and control over someone. These include insults, humiliation, ridicule, silent treatment, and attempts to scare, isolate, and control.

CHAPTER 3

THE SEED OF REJECTION

By the time I was in 5th grade, I had a solid group of friends. We had formed our own group called "DNG." DNG stood for "Dem Naughty Girls." Lol. Back in our day, there was a rap group called The No Limit Soldiers of No Limit Records. The group was made up of some brothers and their friends and family. We loved them. I believed there was a line in one of their songs where we thought they were referring to themselves as "Dem Naughty Boys" so because we loved their music and had crushes on them, we became Dem Naughty Girls. My friend, Taisha, was Mystikal's girl, my friend, Shawanna, was Silkk Da Shocker's girl, I was C-Murder's girl, and our other friends… well I can't remember whose girls they were. Somebody had to be Master P's girl, lol.

For as long as I can remember I always loved Rap/HipHop. The way the lyrics rolled off the tongue of a good rapper was magical to me. If the flow was sick and the beat was hitting when it dropped…I would love it! Rap was my introduction to music, and later I'd fall in love with RnB. The storytelling of music would cause me to get lost in it. I thought that maybe one day I'd be a rapper, lol. EVE was my favorite rapper and when

I was 14, she'd make a song called "Love Is Blind." I would rap this song in the mirror with a brush as my microphone. Ha-ha!

My DNG bffs and I would meet up at the back corner of the playground area for our daily club meetings. Our friend Dee brought us rings from the Piggly Wiggly store, and we wore them every day. If you didn't have one of those rings, then you were NOT allowed in our space! Being with my friends was the best part of my day. They brought so much peace to my life. We were more than friends; they were the sisters I never had. So, because I technically wasn't supposed to be listening to rap music (my grandmother didn't allow it, she thought the lyrics were too vulgar, says the woman whose picture is in the dictionary next to the word CUSS.) I had to sneak and listen to it with my friends. Shawanna would write the lyrics for me so I could learn them & rap along with the crew by the next day's recess, lol. She would turn out to be my best friend and we'd stay connected throughout our adult lives. I took the paper with the lyrics on it, folded it, and put it in my pocket. I forgot all about it because not only were we "rappers," but we were entrepreneurs too, lol. A couple of days a week me and DNG would bring our old toys, things we made, candy, etc., and sell them at recess.

We were making bank! After school, my grandmother must have found the paper in my pocket and read it. She was livid. I got slapped and put on punishment and I was forced to give the paper back. It was so embarrassing! Shawanna already knew how life on Mason Street was, so she didn't trip, and I never heard her clown me for it. I was so mad at my grandmother; I hated being slapped in my face. It felt so degrading, and I didn't understand why I had to be locked up and kept away from everything! I often wished I could just run away. *Haven't seen mama in a while… wonder where she is.* By this time, I had 3 brothers and 1 sister. I figured she wasn't coming for me now; she has a daughter. The next few days were normal except for that punishment. No TV and I couldn't talk to my friends on the phone… it sucked. I was happy to get back to the playground with DNG.

So let me tell you, Mason Street wasn't in a grand rich area. It was in the heart of the hood, and so was my school. There would be drug addicts and homeless people walking directly through the playground. They used the sidewalk that stretched from one end to the other, which connected one side of the neighborhood to the next. This day, my friends and I were waiting for the rest of our friends to come out of the building when we got to the subject of fathers. They lived at home with their mothers and siblings and neither of their fathers lived with them, but they both knew who their fathers were.

When it was my turn to talk about my dad all I could say was, "I don't know who he is." Just as the words rolled off my tongue, here comes a "bum" (that's what we called them as kids) walking up the sidewalk. Taisha looks at me in disbelief and says, "So you're for real, you don't know who your daddy is?"

"No, I never met him" I replied, "so this BUM could be your daddy and you wouldn't even know it." This made me upset, so I fussed with her. "Shut up TAISHA! That's not my dad! Why you always gotta have something smart to say?" She looked at me with a straight face, unfazed by my expression, and said, "…but how do you know though?" I didn't have an answer and that made me furious. The bell rang and it was time to head back inside. Thank God! As I walked home from school that day, my thoughts spoke to me…. LOUDLY. What if my friend was right? What if the homeless guy was my dad? What if my dad was dead? What if he's someone I know? I made up my mind that I needed to find this man. So, the plot began to figure out who and where he was. I knew I'd have to go through my grandmother, and I knew that she wouldn't be happy.

This Lady is going to kill me, I thought as I approached the gate to our yard. "Hey Dani, how was school?" she asked. "Hi, it was good. Awards Day is coming up, and I'm on the Principal's Honor Roll Again, and I'm also getting a Presidential Award for an essay I wrote on helping the homeless," I said while trying to warm up to ask her the big question. "That's good, another one to add to the collection," she said. She always took pleasure in me being on the honor roll and such things like that, and in all honesty, she was the one who helped me with my homework projects and stayed on me to keep on top of my grades. Because of her, I was always on the honor roll, ALWAYS! I had ribbons, awards, pendants, pins, trophies, medals, certificates, all of that. So many award shows had come and gone, and my mother would not be there. I never saw her waiting to hug and take pictures with me as the other student's parents did. My grandmother was always there though.

"Speaking of 'homeless' can I ask you a question?" She answered with a quick yes and a smile. I was almost certain that she thought I was going to ask her for some canned goods to donate to the 'Help Box' at school. "My friends and I were talking today, and they started talking about their fathers and they asked me about my father." I could see her hair standing up on her head. "I told them I didn't know who he was, and Taisha said he could be a bum on the street, and I wouldn't know it. So, I was wondering if you know who he is?" That was the fastest I ever spit a question out of my mouth because I was afraid. In doing it that way she was so busy listening to what I had to say that she didn't have time to curse me out or interrupt. I thought she was about to punch or slap me, or maybe she'd wait until I got in the shower and whoop me with a belt again, she had done that before. Either way, I felt like my question was worth whatever punishment came my way.

She got quiet for a moment and then she finally opened her mouth as if she were expecting me to ask this question eventually. "I don't know him personally, but his name is Ronald. Your mother originally told us that your dad was the boy she was seeing at the time, but I never believed that. He and his mother came to see you one Christmas when you were a baby, and I knew that black a** boy was not your daddy. Eventually, your mother told us the truth that she messed around with this other boy…. he's the son of a Preacher. That's it, that's all I know."

She never said he and his family had lived a couple of blocks away from us my entire life or that the family was well-known in the community. I could tell she knew more…a lot more. I pressed my luck with it and asked her if she could call my mom and tell her I wanted to meet him. She said she would, but I could feel the hurt from her and my granddad, especially my granddad, because I wanted to meet him. At this point, something inside was longing for my parents, almost like calling for them, and I decided since they weren't coming for me, I'd have to look for them. You can imagine my surprise and excitement when a few days later my grandmother told me that on that Saturday my parents were coming to get me to take me to lunch and meet my father. I wanted to cry! I wanted to be super excited! Instead, I said quietly, "ok."

This was on Sunday. In my head, I counted down the days. Lord, please let this week fly by Monday… Tuesday… Wednesday… Thursday… Friday… Saturday… finally! I got up and washed, brushed my teeth and my hair, and put on the cutest outfit I had. I asked her if she could gather some of my awards and ribbons so I could take them to show them. I could tell she didn't want to, but she did. So, I sat on the living room floor with my stack of awards, and I waited… And waited… And waited. I was hungry, but I didn't want to eat because I needed my appetite, so I just waited. Some time had gone by, and I couldn't take it anymore. Just as I was about to knock on my grandparents' door, mommy came flying out. "They not coming." Was what she blurted out. I wanted to collapse, but instead, tears started to roll down my face. A lot of tears. Because my grandmother had been so nice to me during this process, I thought she would console me, but she didn't. Instead, she began screaming! "How dare you, you ungrateful B****, you are crying over them, and they didn't even want your little a**. If it hadn't been for me, you would have been either dragged from house to house like your mama was doing or in foster care. Yeah, your mama originally took you and ran away but we found her hiding at a friend's house with you in the tub. You were dirty, hungry, and I took you, but you see she ain't never come back for you.

Your daddy was a trifling little boy, who ain't try to come for you either. I put my life on hold to raise you and your cousin! Me! Nobody else. Do you think I wanted to raise more kids? I already raised mine and you got the nerve to be crying over them!" I was flabbergasted. My 10-year-old brain was unable to process all of what had just transpired. Something left me that day as the words of her heart were planted into my spirit. I didn't know that she had just placed fertilizer on the top of a seed of rejection that was planted by my parents. I felt so low. I felt like trash that was thrown out of a moving vehicle, and there was not a care in the world about where it landed. That day changed my life, and it would kickstart a lengthy period of low self-esteem, low self-worth, second-guessing myself, internal abuse, and emotional instability. This is where I was open to anger, and I would go inside the shell of myself often. This is where the anxiety and the hurt were birthed from. The seed of rejection was deeply seeded, with its roots choking me, and it would take almost 30 years to break free from it. Until then, I was a pearl inside of a clam, and nobody knew it, not even me.

CHAPTER 4

SAFE HAVENS AND SILVER DOLLAR PANCAKES

Since I was a small girl, I remember going to church every Sunday. We attended Refuge RMUE Church faithfully. By we, I mean Jack and me. I never knew why we went. I just knew those were times to get up, put on a dress, stockings, and "church" shoes, get my hair curled, and ride the church bus. I liked church for the most part, but everything after Sunday school was super long and super boring. The preacher would get up and yell, and the saints would yell back at him. "Preach!" "Hallelujah!" "Amen" and "Yes, sir"! Some of them would even shout and fall out, lol. We would laugh and joke about how silly they looked. My grandparents didn't attend church though. In fact, my grandma never went to church. They were the religious type of people though. They didn't curse on Sundays or listen to "blues," but come Monday, those words were back to normal sailing throughout the house.

Although they didn't attend church, my Aunt Allie did. Aunt Allie was my grandfather's sister. I loved and adored her, and she loved and adored me. She was tall and slender, well dressed, with a cute smile, and she always had her hair and nails done. She was also a licensed cosmetologist and my hairdresser. Every two weeks I'd go with her to work at the salon and she'd either relax or press & curl my hair. I felt like a beautiful princess when I stepped out of her chair. I had long, silky, black hair that would ribbon curl so perfectly! Aunt Allie would also take me sometimes on the weekends to spend the night at her house. I loved it there. I felt so at peace there. I could breathe. She was so nice, soft-spoken, and gentle with me. It's like she knew how fragile I was and handled me with love and care. She'd hug and kiss me and tell me that she loved me. She was a mother too. She had three sons, and her younger son was a few years older than me. His name was Dawayne. He was the best big cousin to Jack and Me and we looked up to him. He was super smart and had plans to be a doctor or something important like that.

Aunt Allie's house was my Safe Haven, my place of refuge and security. The weekends I'd spend with her would always end with her making us silver-dollar pancakes for breakfast on either Saturday mornings or Sunday mornings before church. Even the pancakes were perfect! I called them silver dollar pancakes because she made the small ones close to the size of the silver dollar. We would have girl talk, and she would smile at me. She asked me "Dani-girl, are you OK? Is everything OK in your little world? I so desperately wanted to tell her no, that I hated it at my grandparents' house and how broken up I was about my parents not wanting me, but I was afraid. After all, she's my grandfather's sister. Who would believe me? My grandparents seemed to have everyone fooled. So, I'd nod and smile, and cry silent tears the whole ride home.

At this time, I'd also start spending some weekends at my mother's house. She lived somewhere called "the projects." The energy you felt once you passed the security gates was nothing like Mason Street. The project had a bunch of mini houses with lots of women and lots of kids. The park was packed, and you could smell crabs boiling on Friday nights! Music was playing and the moms gathered on each other's porches. They played cards or just drank and talked. Everyone was having a good time, and I was happy! I got to play with my brothers and even babysit my baby sisters. My sister, Erin, was three and the baby, Alicia, was around one.

My mom also had this guy. His name was "Henry." He was my sister's dad and he'd come home late on Friday nights and be gone all day Saturday, so I rarely interacted with him on visits. He was a truck driver so sometimes he wouldn't be there much at all. There was something strange about him though, and kind of scary. He was very dark-skinned and had a few gold teeth. I kept my distance from him. Until now the only relationship I'd had with a man was with my grandfather, Charlie, so I didn't even know how to talk to another man. I remember a few other guys my mom had dated. There was Todd, who was my three brothers' (Chad, Todd Jr, and Juice's) dad. He was nice, but he and my mom had broken up after years of being together. There was also a guy around named "Kap" when I was young. I was terrified of him! He was a big-time drug dealer, and he kept my mother with the latest fashions and looking cute all the time. He had money and so did Henry. Now that I think about it, my mother dealt with a lot of ballers. One day she came over and I was embarrassed because she had on this colorful, denim-striped booty shorts outfit with the denim vest shirt to match. My mom was a thick woman so all I saw was skin when she walked through the door. I was embarrassed to see her like that, so I turned my head. I heard she was in love with Kap, but he used to fight her; in fact, a lot of her men did. Kap gave me the same creepy vibes as Henry. I didn't want any parts of either of them. Kap and my mother ended up getting arrested on a drug-related situation where the police kicked my mother's door in.

The story has it that my mom didn't have anything to do with it, so Kap took all of his charges and hers. He went to jail for a long time, and he died there before he could get out. It was rumored that he died of AIDS. To me, he was a "real man" for taking those charges, and I think my mother probably loved him for the rest of her life because of it. While visiting my mom on the weekends I also got to see my Aunt Deanna (pronounced Dee-anna). She was my mother's best friend. She lived across the street, and she was also a safe haven. She was tough but sweet and she didn't mind knocking someone out if she had to, but she didn't bother anyone either. Somehow, I always felt safe around her. She didn't seem to look down on me like some other adults, and in my opinion, she was the most real friend my mom had. Denise and Deana, ride or die! Not just friends, but more like sisters. She loved all of my mom's children and my mom loved hers. We ran back and forth from her house to ours. Her door was always open to us and ours to her kids. We'd bust open the door, never knocking, and run in. She'd greet me with a "Hey honey!"

She always seemed happy to see me, and not annoyed by my presence. Deanna was a soldier; you could tell she had been through some things and survived! I heard she had taken my mother under her wings and showed her how to navigate through life. She was a little bit older, so she was the big sister that mom never had, and we all loved her. Although Aunt Deanna was a safe haven, I was still scared to tell her what I was experiencing. I wish someone had asked, but back then it was "don't ask don't tell" and everyone just minded their own business. The weekends would end and the feelings of rejection, and abandonment all came back to me on those car rides back to Mason Street. I wish I could just yell and ask my mom to love me and to keep me and not return me to Mason Street. I shed tears in the car and opened my mouth to scream, but nothing would come out. I wish my mom could see that I was hurting and that every time she dropped me off it was like ripping a Band-Aid off of an unhealed cut, exposing the bruise over and over again, but she didn't, or at least she never said a word about it if she did. I dried up my tears and tried to put on a smiling face, but each time it would end the same.

When my mother would pull off, I'd go inside and get cussed out for "looking sad." You always come back here with this SH**. That's why I don't like your A** going over there! If she wanted you, she would have kept you, so fix your face and get it together before I bust your a** and give you something to be sad about." I was crushed and screaming on the inside. I would look at Jackson and he'd have a sad look on his face. It was like he was saying, "Please don't go." I was stuck, hurt, and BROKEN and each time this would occur I'd have to wait longer amounts of time to go back to her house. I wish she had loved me enough to pack up our things and move me and Jack to her house, but I knew that would never happen. By that time, my mother had five other children, and there was no room for me and Jack at her house, and no room in her heart. Slowly I was starting to resent her.

CHAPTER 5

FEELING SOME TYPE OF WAY

I got my first menstrual cycle shortly after I turned 11. I was dumbfounded because no one had ever discussed with me exactly what it was. I vaguely remember my health teacher teaching on the topic, but I still wasn't fully aware of what it was, what it meant, or what was happening to my body. I just remember my grandmother saying if you see blood, let me know. As soon as I told her, she told me what to do. I heard her on the phone with my mother. "Yeah, Denise it happened girl, mmm hmmm. I know right, a little lady now." To myself, I thought, *What are y'all so happy about? I'm the one who must take a shower every time I change my pad! What am I going to do when I have to go to school, and why am I bleeding, am I cut?* The whole thing puzzled me. I asked my grandmother all these questions and she gave me some clarity. Although I didn't fully understand, I felt a lot better after that. My grandmother handed me the phone with my mom on the other end. She said, "Hey Dani, girl you got your cycle OKKKK, I got mine at 11, too." We chatted for a couple of minutes and then we hung up.

Have you ever felt like you had a sixth sense? Like you knew things or could sense things? It was around this time that I started feeling some type of way about things and having weird feelings about my grandfather. My grandfather, Charlie, started working for a local college in downtown Jamestown called The College of Jamestown. I thought he was a teacher or professor, so you can imagine my excitement when I was told that I was going to work with him. He'd hold my hand and we'd walk to the bus stop. I was starting to dislike the hand-holding. It was okay when I was a little girl, but being in the fifth grade, it felt weird. The kids looked at me funny when he walked me to school. It was beginning to be embarrassing. That coupled with the fact that we had to kiss them goodbye on their cheeks just made me feel weird. I didn't see any of the other kids doing that to their parents, but I also didn't want to hurt their feelings, so I didn't make a big deal about it. It was just starting to feel like a girlfriend and boyfriend, and I felt disgusting. One day I went to work with my grandfather, and he went to get his equipment. It was a rolling cart with cleaning supplies and a trashcan on it. I realized that he was a part of the sanitation team. I had seen those types of workers before at my school.

It was cool with me though, I liked to clean! I especially liked that on our cleaning route was a huge auditorium and when I'd help him clean the chairs and floors, I got to keep the money I found there! I used that change at the gas station on our way to the bus stop in the afternoon when it was time to go home. I couldn't wait till next Saturday to get some more change! Boom, the week flies by and I'm back at work! We cleaned, and I found some money! I scraped some gum off the seat, and BAM, there's five dollars. I was so happy because this meant I could have money for ice cream at school the next day. All the cool kids had money for ice cream at school! My cousin Ky would always buy me ice cream when I didn't have any money. That day we got done early and Granddaddy Charles and I walked to the closet where he kept his cleaning cart. Instead of pushing the cart in the closet like usual, we both walked inside. He put a chair against the door and sat in it. He told me to sit down on this little stool, and not to make any noise, he rested his head and back in the chair up against the door and turned the lights off.

As the closet got pitch black, I tried to adjust my sight to the darkness. All I could think was, *God, I hope he doesn't touch me, please don't let him touch me.* The next thing I remember is that there was some noise outside the door which caused him to wake up from his nap and cut the light on. We walked out of the closet when no one was in the area and headed to the bus stop. I blacked out in the closet, and I have no recollection of how long we were there or what happened while we were there. All I remember was darkness. After that weird experience, I didn't want to go back to work with him. I don't remember going back too much after that day either.

I started to feel strange at home too. The TV was set up on one side of the living room and the couch on the other. This left the walkway between the TV and the person sitting on the couch. I felt like when I walked past the TV, Granddaddy Charles was watching me, and it gave me chills and it creeped me out. *Why was I feeling this way?* Again, I didn't have anyone to talk to about it. Things were changing with Jack too. He seemed soft and timid especially around Granddaddy Charles. Charles seemed like he liked to pick on him. He hit him harder than necessary, and he found stuff to be angry with him about. I used to feel so bad. In fact, when he cried, I cried with him, I'd sneak and give him a hug or grab his hand. It was a silent language between us kind of to let him know that he would be OK and that I was with him. Charles would do perverted things too, especially when my brothers came over. He said, "Y'all act up and I will squeeze those little willies." This was referring to their private parts! Or he would do humiliating things like pull Jack's pants down when he was standing at the kitchen sink. Once he nailed my brother Juice to the floor by his pants. He disguised it as humor, but it always seemed like bullying or some sort of scare tactic. I could tell my mother didn't like it because she made a comment to Daddy and asked him to please stop doing that. Before he could answer, my grandmother spoke up loudly, "Oh, Denise, please he not gonna hurt them kids." My mother didn't say anything, but her face got red, and shortly after, she grabbed the boys and left. No goodbyes to Jack and me this time… Again, we were left behind. It was OK, we were used to it, and we knew that no one was coming to get us.

My Auntie Nikki used to come by and bring her kids from time to time. We loved playing with our cousins. I was the only girl in the family for eight years until my sister was born, but she hardly came over to our house. My Auntie Nikki had a daughter who was eight years younger than me too. She came to stay on Mason Street for a short while, but her

mother came and got her. She grew up with her siblings. Poor Jack…
Paris had gotten addicted to the street life and drugs, and Jack rarely saw
his mom. She only came by when she needed a hot plate or a few dollars.
She didn't even seem to notice or care about Jack and me. My Auntie
Nikki ended up living within walking distance, and my grandparents
would let us walk over to spend time at her house. It was fun, but dang
my aunt could yell, and curse! Every word was a cuss word, even more
than at my house on Mason Street, but I guess my cousins were used to
it.

During this period of my life, I was unaware of what homosexuality
was. I knew that it wasn't prevalent, but I had heard that my Auntie Paris
had a girlfriend. That was strange to me and made me wonder if my
childhood friend Reese from kindergarten liked girls. All I knew was that
I didn't like girls in that way! I was starting to wonder about Jack though
because people would tease him at church and call him "GAY." I would
defend him and tell them to leave him alone, and he would run off
behind the church and cry or play by himself. I hated that for him. *Why
won't people just leave him alone?* My thoughts and opinions toward Jack
stayed the same until one day I saw something that I wish I had never
seen. The owners of the house had decided to renovate the house on
Mason Street a couple of years prior, so we no longer had to go through
my grandparents' room. They sealed off the door in their room, tore
down the heater that warmed our butts for so many years, and made a
long hallway. They split our old room in half and made it into two smaller
rooms. I now had my own room and so did Jack.

The dungeon became half of Jack's room and the other half on the opposite side of a wall they built. That other half was now a part of a big walk-in bathroom with a laundry room right off it. We had never had a washer and dryer before. We always walked our clothes to the laundromat in front of the neighborhood. I loved it there too. I found money in the washer and the dryer. Lol. Anyway, my grandmother used to watch a family member's child named Jamal, from time to time. He and Jack were around the same age. I thought that would be good for Jack to have a friend to play with. One particular day I was coming down the hall. My grandmother was in her room with her door closed and Granddaddy Charles was at work. As I approached the end of the hall, I saw Jack laying on his back with his legs up and Jamal on top of him moving in a humping motion. I pulled back and peeked around the corner to make sure I was seeing correctly. Yes, they were grinding on each other, and I wanted to puke. They had to be about 9 or 10 years old. I couldn't see what their faces were doing because I was behind them. I was mad, shocked, and confused. At that moment all I could think about was if my grandmother opened the door, they both were done; so, I acted like I was walking down the hall and shuffled my feet so they could hear me coming. I heard them scramble to sit down, and I walked around the corner. We all acted like nothing happened. I never asked Jack about it. I just knew that Jack was homosexual from that moment, and so was Jamal… That weird feeling came over me again. The one that I had at nap time that day, the one that I had in the closet with Granddaddy Charles, and the one that I had when I felt like eyes were watching me as

I passed the TV. *What was this feeling?* I didn't know what it was then, but that was the feeling of perversion. That spirit was all around me, and in a few years, I would find out just how much.

CHAPTER 6

CHANGES

My 13th birthday was approaching, and I was so excited. Up until now, I had never had a birthday party outside of cake and ice cream with cousins and family so you can imagine my excitement when my mother said she was having a weekend sleepover birthday party for me! I invited all my closest friends. All of DNG was there except Dee. It was me, Taisha, Shawanna, Brianna, and Kay. For the most part, we had a great time. We ate pizza, chilled in the neighborhood, got our nails done, played on people's phones, played games, and just laughed! Our friend Kay had something like extra skin on her toe, which made it look like an extra toe. Taisha, always being the one to mess with somebody, started picking on her about it. We all laughed until I saw that Kay didn't like it. Tears welled up in her eyes and I said, "Ok y'all, let's stop." But the girls didn't stop right away. I always felt bad, like I should've stuck up for her a little more. Eventually, the joke stopped, and we finished the weekend off. I had the best time I'd ever had in my life. It made more of a difference that I got to share the experience with my mom. She was just so great to me, always so nice. She never raised her voice; she was sweet and very motherly. Of course, I didn't want the weekend to end.

I don't remember a whole lot of hugs from my mom, but this time she got out of the car and hugged and kissed me, her red lipstick stuck to my face. As she said goodbye, I whispered "thank you" into her ear. I ran into the house and cried, but I tried my best to clean up before my grandmother got into the house, and then I watched her car pull off again. I think this was the worst goodbye. I was getting older and the longing to be with my mom and siblings was turning into an ache that I couldn't shake anymore. I decided that this was the last time I was going to be dropped off. This was on a Sunday, so school was the next day. I went to school thinking about my decision, I told my best friend that I was going to ask to live with my mother. She was happy for me and said I should go for it. Again Monday… Tuesday… Wednesday… Thursday… Finally, it was Friday! It was time to make my move… I went home and asked my grandmother if I could speak to her. "Mommy, I just really want to say thank you for all that you've done for me. I know if it weren't for you and Granddaddy Charles, I would probably be in foster care and I'm grateful to you for the care you showed me." She was smiling as I expressed my gratitude for all they had done. "I think it's time for me to go and live with my mom though, I would like to do that, and I hope it's ok with you?" Her smile slowly drew back and hurt set in her eyes followed by anger across her face. *What was I thinking? She's about to beat me to the ground!* It wasn't her fist that hit me. It was her words that made me feel like I'd been punched in the gut.

"You mean to tell me after everything we've done for your little ungrateful a** you wanna do this? How dare you? You just wanna go live with your mother because you see how she dresses your brothers. You want shoes and clothes, huh? That's what it is, right? You are a user and you have used us up and now you want to run over there to your mother. Well, I don't care, pack your sh** and get out! You're stupid. Your mama ain't even asked for you!" At this point, I was very shocked. I started to go to my room, then I heard her voice say, "no, in fact, don't touch nothing. I'm about to walk you to Denise's house. She got dressed so fast that I didn't even get to say goodbye to Jack.

My grandfather just stood in the doorway looking out of it into the street. When we walked out, I stopped and hugged him. He didn't say anything. She unlocked the lock on the gate, and we walked out of it. I had unlocked and walked out of those doors and gates a million times, but this time was different. This time didn't seem real, it seemed like it was a dream. It almost felt like I was walking away from everything I knew and walking into the unknown. On that walk that I had walked a million times before, the streets and the buildings felt so much bigger this time around. Beyond the walls, sealed windows, locked doors, and chained gates of Mason Street seemed very unsheltered. A wave of fear and nervousness came over me and I asked myself if I was doing the right thing.

My grandmother didn't speak to me for the entire walk. This made the usual 20-minute walk to the projects feel like a two-day trip. I heard a sniffle every few steps though. *Was what I did bad?* I didn't know then, but this was all manipulation. We reached my mother's door. Apparently, Mommy had called my mom because she didn't look surprised when we showed up. My grandmother didn't say a word, I walked in the door, and she turned around and walked away. I looked at my mom, and then I looked out the screen door at my grandmother as she walked away. I felt so torn between the two. I really wasn't trying to hurt anyone. Then I felt my mother's hands on my shoulders. She pulled me away from the door and shut it. "Don't worry about her, she'll be fine." I never heard my mother say a bad word about my grandparents, but the look on her face was of both sadness and disgust. She walked away silently. I put my purse down and walked around the house looking for my brothers and sisters. So, apparently, my sibs were never home on the weekends. My brothers were with their dad and my sisters were with their godmother. That left me and my mom. Finally, the moment for which I'd been waiting. We went to her room, and she started talking and telling me how she never intended to leave me behind. She told me the story of how she ran with me, and her parents found us hiding at a friend's house in their tub. They said if you wanna be out here living from house to house, you go ahead, but this baby will not, and then they took me away from her.

She said she went back home for a little while to stay with me but couldn't take it anymore and when I turned two, she left and never came back. "The plan was to come back for you. I never meant to leave you there for good."

"What happened? How did I end up staying?" I asked. "By the time I tried to come back, you were already attached to them. You'd cry when

I picked you up to spend the night and I'd have to send you back or Granddaddy Charles would come by to 'check' on you and when you saw him you cried to go back with him. He knew that you would do that, so I think he did it on purpose."

I had so many questions, but I didn't want to overwhelm her while she was sharing those things with me. My biggest question at the time was why were you running away from home? I couldn't find the words to ask, although I really wish I had. I went to bed that night and cried a few tears before falling asleep. The tears were for my grandparents, they had done a number on me because I was so concerned that I hurt them. Why should I be sad? I didn't do anything wrong! Life was about to change for me in many ways, I just didn't know how much more. I woke up and my mother told me to get dressed and that we were going shopping and to get breakfast. I was excited again! I remembered the times my mom would pick me and Jack up. She had taken us to this place called The Fox. It was a movie theater with an arcade inside of it; she took us to Chuck E. Cheese a couple of times and to the public pool. We always had such great times.

I got dressed, and as I walked out of the room I walked straight into Henry as he was walking out of my mother's room. When did he get here? My mother was all smiles, so I guess it was cool. We hopped into his car and went to Mammy's for breakfast. Then we headed to the tent. The tent was a popular spot on the corner of G-Road that people shopped at. I got a cute dress and a short pants outfit. After that, Henry dropped my mom off to get her car. He left and we went to the beauty store. I bought lip gloss and some sandals. After that, we went home and got dressed. I put on one of my outfits and my new sandals, and we headed to Cherry Hill. I found out that Henry's family met up at his people's house on Saturdays for cookouts and drinks. That's when I met Laysha. Laysha was Henry's niece and we immediately clicked. We already knew we were cousins because her brother Ky was in my fifth-grade class. We knew we were related because my grandfather had told us one day at school. Everybody on Cherry Hill was his family. That's the street he was born and raised on. Aunt Allie also lived on that street. So did my grandfather's aunt, uncle, and cousin. His childhood home was still there also and owned by the family. Now I'm confused because if these people are Granddaddy Charles' cousins doesn't that make them my mother's cousins too? *What was my mother doing? Did she have two kids with her cousin?* Here I go again with the questions, I told myself to chill. I was sure there was an explanation for all of this.

The bond grew deeper as Laysha and I spent the summer together. She and my mom were close too. We took turns spending the night/weekend at each other's houses. Laysha's house reminded me of Mason Street a little. They had bars on their windows and locks on their doors and gates. Her mom was a little on the stern side, but I guess she had her good days too. Laysha, as well as my other friends loved to spend the night at my house because living in the projects was fun and "amp." My friends came over and the first thing we'd do was walk down the hill. We would go to the park, walk to one of our other friends' houses, go to the candy store, walk to the front gate, go to the hair store, and back to the hood. Along the way, we'd stop to talk to all the homies and go back up the hill. Sometimes we hung out on the sidewalk at the top of the hill. There were always kids our age outside. It was fun and everybody got along, all the mothers watched out for everyone else's kids. It was like a family, and I loved the fact that I got to go outside every day. This was such a positive change for me. I became more social, and a little sure of myself, and I made friends fast. People who I still communicate with today. I made friends with guys my age too. It always seems so much easier to have guys as friends, there was no drama Lol. I just considered myself the homie who happened to be a girl! By this time, my friends had developed crushes on some of the guys around my neighborhood. None of us were "fast' as I heard the ladies on the porch say. Everyone still had their virginity, because why wouldn't we? We were only 13 years old, but by this time I did start to hear things from girls in the neighborhood or the bathroom at school about sex.

Neither my mother nor my grandparents had ever talked to me about it before and all the kids were talking about it so much I started to get curious. Still not curious enough to try it though… but I had started to be interested in boys. A trip to the park one summer day would be when I met my first "boyfriend." I mean I had had crushes on boys before, but nothing serious. I went to the park like usual, and I noticed this kid looking at me. I looked up and he smiled and said, "What's up?" The amount of base in his voice was scary. I said, "What's up" and the conversation started. "You're Chad's big sister, right?" "Yeah, I am" "Where you been at all this time?" "I used to live with my grandparents,"

I replied. "What's your name?" he continued "My name is Dani, Dani with an I, what's yours?" "Tre" he answered. "Well, it's nice to meet you Tre." He asked if I wanted him to walk me home and I told him that was fine. He was on a bike, so I walked, and he peddled beside me. We walked and talked, and I even laughed. He had such a radiant smile; with the whitest teeth I'd ever seen up until that point. His skin was like smooth Black Silk. As we approached my house, I saw my mom in the doorway.

She had an agitated look on her face. I think Tre saw it too because he split before we got completely up the hill. Things had started changing at my house too. It seems like my mother and Henry had started arguing and fighting more often. I would hear my mother fussing about other females and things of that sort. They had often been fighting physically too. My mother seemed sadder, and I thought maybe that was why she was angry this day, but I was wrong. When I got to the door she said "I don't want you getting caught up with these boys. You are not allowed to have a boyfriend, do you understand?" I said yes, but I really didn't understand. I wish she had sat me down and explained to me why I couldn't have a boyfriend, but she didn't. Eventually, I started sneaking around to see Tre, including meeting him at my sister's god-sister's house. My mother found out and was angry with both me and her. As the "relationship" continued, my mother didn't have to tell me to leave Tre alone. He started to become violent. One day he told me to come over to him and when I didn't, he grabbed me by the arm and jacked me up. "Didn't I tell you to come here? You come when I call you." I had seen my mother be in an abusive relationship, so I not only knew the signs, but I also knew that I didn't want to be in one. I broke up with him, and as we grew older, I heard stories of how he grew up to be abusive in his relationships. I thank the lord that I was able to come out of that relationship early! Maybe Mama was right. I thought about telling her about it, but she was going through her own relationship and inner battles to be who I needed her to be in that moment, so I just let her be.

CHAPTER 7

DADDY'S GIRL?

Living with mama was great but my expectation of me and her building this perfect bond was slowly ending. It seemed so hard to connect. There were a lot of factors that contributed to that. I just believed everything would work itself out. One day we were talking, and I decided to ask her about my father. She explained how they met in middle school and were never really dating. "Yeah, your dad and I really liked each other, but we kind of hooked up before anything could become of a relationship. We were very young." Until now I had never known that my mother and I only had a 15-year age gap between us. "I got pregnant with you when I was 14 years old. I ended up telling my friend I was pregnant and that your dad was the father. Before I could tell him, she told him or someone else and they told him, and one day he got on the school bus and threatened me to stop saying I was pregnant for him, or he was going to beat me up!" My mouth was wide open. She continued "I was scared, and I never mentioned it to your dad again. I had a boyfriend, and he was willing and wanting to be your father. He and his mom came by a few times after you were born and brought gifts, but my mother and his mother looked at you and realized you weren't his. We ended up breaking up and my mother made me tell her who your father was. Your dad's family was a well-known family in the area, so she knew exactly who I was talking about. We never went to his family though; we just raised you ourselves." After hearing this I didn't even know what to think or say. That was a very grown-up situation to have to face at 14/15 and this was a very grown-up situation to place on me at 13. That's what I got for asking. My questions always led to answers I wasn't ready for! So, no fairytale love story, I was just an unwanted mistake that happened at the house party!!

I think I started to feel even worse about myself. Then she would go on to say how she had two friends who both attended the family church and had told her that she should take me to the church. She was conflicted about doing that because she didn't want to just show up on these people's doorstep or in this case church step with me. She asked me what I thought. I told her we should go. Nobody was going to know who we were. What's the worst that can happen? Here comes the month of May and there's a special service coming up that we were told would be a great Sunday for us to come. The day came and we got ready. Back then, my friends and I used to line our lips with a black lip liner and shine them with gloss. I did that and put on a black & white dress. I was extremely nervous but like I said, who's going to know me, we could sneak in and sneak out no big deal! I was wrong… Real wrong! We got to the church and sat down. I immediately started looking around, while Mama's friend was whispering to me who was who. "That's your aunt... that's your uncle... that right there is your cousin and that is your grandmother. I remembered looking at the woman who was dressed in all black and thinking "Wow, she's a pretty lady." Just then a chunky, light-skinned kid, looking to be a little younger than me, walked into the pulpit. He began his sermon, and I watched him "preach" while the people cheered. He was like a little mini preacher. I watched my grandmother clap and shout as he preached harder. I had never seen a kid in a pulpit before.

Mama's friend said, "That is your cousin, David Jr ." I didn't know, but I was looking at my first cousin, and over the years we became close and more like brother and sister. I watched him finish his sermon and step down from the pulpit. There was an elderly man in a wheelchair, and I saw people paying homage to him. "Who is that?" I asked Mom's friend. That is Bishop. He's your great-grandfather, your dad's grandfather." I thought to myself how I wish I had known these people back in kindergarten because then my family tree would have been able to be full. "Ok, where is my dad? Is he not here?" Just then, she said, "Your daddy's not here." A small wave of disappointment came over me when she said it. My mother squeezed my hand and said "Dani, it's OK don't worry about it. We'll find him." Church ended and everybody started hugging and talking. I looked at my mom who had this nervous look on her face. *What do we do now?* I thought to myself. *Do we walk out... ? Yes, that's what we need to do. Just walk out.* For some reason, neither mine nor my mother's feet would move. I noticed this man wearing a gray suit and a huge smile walking toward us. He was greeting and hugging everyone as he walked our way. He looks up at my mama and says, "Denise, is that you?" I'm thinking to myself, *wait who is this guy, and why does he seem to know my mother?* He looked a lot like my cousin David Jr. "Yes, it's me, how are you, how have you been? It's been a long time since I've seen you." I don't recall if anyone ever said the words, "This is Ron's daughter," to him. I'm almost 99.9% sure that no one did. He opened his arms and gave me the warmest hug that I ever had.

"Hey baby, I'm your Uncle David. I'm your Daddy's big brother!" I hugged him back, smiled, and said, "Hi nice to meet you." In that moment a feeling of love and I don't know, I guess acceptance came over me. It felt so real and not rehearsed, not expected but real RAW emotion. It almost felt like he had known me all my life and was waiting for me. I imagined that this was what it would be like when I met my dad! As soon as he let me go, the woman who was said to be my grandmother was behind him. He said "Ma, this is Ronald's daughter, Dani." She opened her arms wide and had tears in her eyes. She hugged me deeply, and I felt like I got lost in her dress. She said, "I'm your grandmother," to which I smiled and responded "Hi." She, too, seemed like she was expecting me. That would be the end of the warm welcomes for that day, though.

My grandmother, who was an evangelist, walked me over to the Bishop as he sat in his chair. "Daddy, this is Ron's daughter." He took a long look at me and paused. Everyone who stood around got quiet and waited for his response. After a few seconds, he said, in a low, raspy voice, "I told these boys about spreading my seeds all around." Everyone smiled and laughed and somehow, I felt like that was his approval. The last group I was taken to was a group of my aunts. One aunt was standing inside the church, and I was never really introduced to her. She was standing there, doing something when my uncle said to somebody else, "This is Ron's daughter!" The Auntie said, "Oh we don't know that, yet." I heard someone shush her and she said, "I'm just saying we don't know that yet." It felt awkward and I can imagine how my mom felt. I remember thinking, *ok she must be the mean auntie*, lol. It turns out she would be the cool auntie who just didn't mind speaking her mind. We got to know each other, I grew to love and respect her, and she grew to love and respect me. To this day she's the one I'm closest to.

Lastly, I was taken outside on the porch and the other three sisters were standing in a circle. They looked like some type of singing group. It also looked like they were having a conversation. which reduced them to talking with their eyes when I walked up. Uncle David said, "Y'all this is Ron's daughter!" One of the aunts said hi. She was the youngest. The middle aunt just stared. She never said hi or anything, she just looked at me like I was invisible, and the older of the three aunts gave me a low hi. It was an unsure hi, like I'm not sure if this is my brother's child kind of hi. I felt such a cold feeling on the porch that day, even though it was summertime… Uncle David must've felt it too because he looked and then directed me back into the church to find my mother. We ended up running into David Jr. He was standing there, staring at me with a "look." My uncle said that's my son, David Jr. I'm David Senior. I knew they looked alike. David Jr. never said a word either, he just stood there staring, like he was looking through my soul. Later, after we became close, he would tell me, "I was looking like who is this girl with all this black liner on her lips, you were pretty, but that liner was just too much." We laughed, and I wondered if that's what the aunts were staring at too! The last person Uncle introduced me to was Deacon Chip. The guy had the widest smile I'd ever seen, and he looked very scary. Note to self: *stay away from this guy*. Uncle David said, "This is my pops," and I was like, *oh great this guy is my grandfather*. As it would turn out, Uncle David was just really close with the guy, so he was like a father figure to him.

So where was my grandfather? I never met him that day. Then that was it. My mom and I got into our car, and she asked me what I thought and how I felt. I smiled and said that was a lot of people, lol. The crazy thing is that wasn't even half. We talked and laughed all the way home, and it was one of the better times between me and her. I loved that we had times like this, just me and her talking and laughing. She seemed genuinely happy for me to have met my family. The last thing I said to her was, "Yep this was good, now it is time to find my dad." My mother said, "ok I will find him." May was ending and June was approaching. I wondered how long it would be before I met him, I was starting to think he lived in China, but I learned that a man who didn't want to be found was hard to find. Weeks went by but it felt more like months. My mom called me into the living room and said so calmly, "I spoke to your dad, and he wants to come pick you up on Sunday and take you to church with him." I didn't know what to say, for the first time I was internally speechless. I just said, "ok." I think I was shocked more than anything, Shocked that it was happening, shocked that he existed, just shocked! Suddenly, I wasn't sure I wanted to go through with it. It was almost too late as it was already Wednesday, and he was coming on Sunday. I figured that I needed to get it together. I went into my closet and picked out a yellow dress. It was a soft canary yellow, and I thought it looked pretty on my skin. My hair was in braids, so I decided I would put it in a bun. *Ok Sunday, let's go, I'm ready!* Sunday morning came and I was ready and nervous.

I watched the greyish-champagne-colored van pull up to the sidewalk and a tall, slender man got out. His hair was cut low, but it was very thick, black, and wavy. He looked so young to me, almost like he could pass for my older brother. Technically he could, he was only 16 years older than me. He walked up to the door, and I walked out. He said, 'Hi, how are you doing?" I said "Hi. I'm doing fine." He was just as nervous as me. We walked up to the car, and he grabbed the door handle and slid the back door open. I was surprised to see three pairs of eyes looking at me. There was a lady in the front, a baby girl, and a young girl in the backseat. The baby didn't know what was going on. She just looked and blinked. The little girl gave me a nasty look like I stunk, and the woman smiled and said, "Hi, I'm Shanda." She was pretty with blonde hair and the girls were cute too. I thought to myself, *ohhh he must be giving someone a ride to church.* That happened often back then. When a member of the church was having car trouble or without transportation, someone would give them a ride. That was nice of him to pick up this lady and her kids. Then she continued, "I'm Ronald's wife." *What? Why? When? Huh?* Nobody said anything about him being married or having children! I felt confused and I wanted to go back inside. Instead, I said

"Nice to meet you." I got into the car, but I couldn't believe it. How was I supposed to build a relationship with my dad when he already had a family? It just seemed like no matter how hard I tried I would never be number one to anyone, even though technically I was number one! The first daughter and the first granddaughter on both sides. Then I thought to myself *calm down you're worried for nothing. Give these people a chance, I mean, his wife seemed nice. He seemed nice and besides nothing was going to happen. These are church people.* I looked up and saw that my dad kept looking at me through the rearview mirror. He would smile each time our eyes connected, then I looked over and the older of the two girls was looking at me. She turned up her nose and cut her eyes before turning to look out the window. *Yeah Dani, this is going to be a long day…*

We pulled up to the church and I think I was expecting it to look like the small churches I was used to. Instead, it was like some type of warehouse building. People stared at me like I was foreign. I guess they were wondering who I was. We went to our seats and the people were on the stage singing with tracks. I was looking for a choir or a band. My dad was playing the drums and I thought that was cool because I had always wanted to play the drums or the acoustic guitar. Maybe he could teach me. I sat through the service. It was very commercial, no soul, no whooping and hollering, and no organ. Definitely not what I was used to. After church Shanda walked me around and introduced me as "Dani, Ronald's daughter," putting extra emphasis on "Ronald 's daughter." The people she was introducing me to appeared to be shocked, and some even looked like they could care less. Some looked like they sympathize with her. It gave "poor you having to deal with an outside child" vibes. By the time it was time to meet the pastor I was over it. He smiled, hugged me, and said, "nice to meet you."

After we left church that day, we attended a Father's Day cookout at my grandmother 's house. I walked in and saw all the people that I had seen at the church the day my mom and I met the family. Everyone seemed happy to see me. My grandmother gave me a big hug and said "Hi It's nice to see you again. The house was full of cousins to play with, but I was very shy, so I spent most of the time sitting in the den. My dad and I both went to change clothes and when we came out, we were dressed alike. We both came out wearing white T-shirts and denim overalls, which everyone thought was so cute especially after they found out that it wasn't planned. I don't know how his wife felt but she didn't look so happy. One of my aunts started pointing out the similarities between my dad and me. We were both "Bo-legged" and I was a bit pigeon toed. Apparently, my father, my father's twin brother, my grandmother, and my grandfather all had the same traits. They laughed about how the twins had to wear braces on their legs when they were younger and the sound that they would make when they came running to the dinner table. Everyone laughed, and my dad told joke after joke. They continued to point out our similarities and my shyness kicked into overdrive, so eventually I eased back into the den. Being in adults' company felt strange to me. I wasn't used to that because we weren't allowed to be in adult company at my grandparents' house.

I heard them laughing and joking, they seemed like a really nice family, and for most of my childhood, they would be. However, I would find out that things are not always what they seem. My dad dropped me off at home that night and gave me a hug for the first time. It was awkward, and it didn't feel quite like the hug Uncle David gave to me, but nevertheless, I took it for what it was, and I thought to myself this is the moment I've been waiting for, but I didn't know that in the years to come there would be times that I wished I had never gone looking for him.

CHAPTER 8

LOSING

Meeting my dad was cool but it didn't provide me with what I needed. He was very quiet and didn't communicate well, and when he would say something, it would come out very arrogantly and without remorse. I was shy and didn't know how to express myself. This was a recipe for disaster. I spent a lot of time at their house during the summer. I went there on Wednesdays and stayed till Saturday. I would babysit my sisters for them while they were at work. I'm not going to lie I didn't like staying there. I missed my friends. I missed hanging out at the park. I missed having fun. It was boring at my father's house. Babysitting for them was cool, and they even paid me, but I couldn't go outside to play, and we were alone most of the day until they got home. I also really didn't like going to church with them. It was clear that I wasn't like the people there. I really felt like an outsider and even though I now knew who my dad was, it seemed like we really couldn't bond the way we needed to because there was always someone around. We started staying up late at night when I stayed over. We ate ice cream and talked. Those times were really nice except for the times Shanda would want him to come upstairs to bed. I was starting to feel like she was trying to control how far our relationship went or maybe it was jealousy that his time had to be divided with the daughter he shared with someone else. I remember the time when my dad said, "You're my daughter you can sit on my lap." He was referring to the fact that the other two girls had sat on his lap. His wife came running out of the kitchen saying, "No she cannot! Don't you think she's a little too old for that?" We all just got silent, and my dad shook his head in disgust…

I never sat on his lap, nor did I feel comfortable doing anything else for a while. I think that the moment when he was trying to make me feel accepted and equal with the other girls was stolen from him. He never mentioned it again. The relationship I had hoped to have with my dad was far from the relationship we seemed to be building. We had a lot in common, but the connection was hard to reach. There was a sense of validation that I was looking for, validation that I needed, which he was not able to give. After a while, he seemed to only equate fatherhood to discipline. I thought that was kind of out-of-pocket for him. He was not in my life by his own choice, and he didn't even try to look for me, nor did he seem to care about me or my well-being, wherever it was that I was being raised. I started internally, blaming him for everything that I had experienced in my life. Feelings of rejection plagued me heavily. Now, thinking back to some of my behaviors, I realize all the signs were there. Everyone was just too caught up with their own problems to stop and ask me what I felt or what I needed.

<><><><><><>

My parents expected me to jump into the stage of life we were in and not hold them accountable for what they had done to me. All of this caused me to become angry, and eventually, I started rebelling against them. Dear Reader, rebellion is NOT OK! Rebellion is the exact spirit Satan operated in, which caused him to be kicked out of heaven. If you are rebelling against your parents or any authority, I advise you to seek God, ask him to deliver you, and pray that if indeed you are being mistreated by those authoritative figures, that he "turns the heart of the king in your favor" and cause them to treat you like the jewel you are. BUT remember, PSALM 27:10 "When my father and mother forsake me, then the Lord will take care of me…"

Often when a child displays behavioral issues there is some type of troubling experience that contributes to the reason for the behavior. Not an excuse for the behavior, but absolutely a reason! This is when I feel like I began a season of "Losing." I started my eighth-grade year at Nightside Middle School. I was excited to be with my friends again after a year at military school. I was doing well but my focus and my concentration were off. I found myself getting upset more frequently and more quickly than usual. Most of the time it was built up frustration about what was going on at home and with my father. By that time, it seemed like my mom and I just couldn't see eye to eye. I was starting to get the feeling that she didn't even really like me. It was trivial things at first, like how mad she always seemed. I guess she was going through a lot emotionally. due to her relationship, but I was a kid and didn't understand. I didn't understand her, and she didn't understand me. I didn't know that there was a little girl inside of her crying for help too. I didn't know. She was incapable of being a fully functionally emotionally sound mother because she didn't have one.

Cycles of abuse are detrimental to the generational downlines because if the generation before doesn't get delivered, the abuse patterns subconsciously pass down to the next, and it keeps repeating. This is what a cycle is. A series of events that are regularly repeated in the same order. If you're reading this here's your chance to recognize when you are in a negative generational cycle and break free from it. Free yourself and the next generation by becoming a GCB! I am a Generational Curse Breaker!

Now looking back, I think we both were losing, but couldn't see past our own issues to give the other grace. I remember the night things changed between us forever. My mom and her friend went out and left me and my friend at the house. Mama had stopped me from hanging out outside so much, so we knew to stay inside. As we were sitting in the living room waiting for them to come back, in walked Henry. He had a grin on his face, and I knew something was up. Most of the time he was drunk, "What's up Dani?" he said to me; and I responded with a dry, "Sup Henry." Instead of keeping it moving and leaving us alone he decided to stop and take a little look at me. Then he said, "Oh you ain't had those when you first got here, they getting big." Then he laughed. I asked him what he was talking about, and he pointed at my chest. I looked at him with squinted eyes and a turned-up nose, but before I could say anything my friend grabbed my hand and pulled me outside onto the porch. She said, "Let's just wait for our mothers out here."

"Great idea because I don't feel comfortable in the house with him." He was such a jerk. About 20 minutes later, my mom and her friend pulled up. Immediately, she starts going in on me.

"Why are you outside my door at this time of night, didn't I tell you to stay in the house?" My friend then said to her, "Denise, Dani got something to tell you." With that I proceeded to tell her what happened and when I was done, she and her friend went to the house. I could hear her fussing at Henry "Why did you say that to Dani?" "I was just saying how she's grown since she's been here, that's all I meant," he replied. "No, that is unacceptable. You don't say that to her, that is very inappropriate." They exchanged a few more words, and then he left. My mother called us inside and said that she believed what I said because there were rumors of him messing around with a girl close to my age. Her friend goes on further to say "Yeah, because he said he'll never turn down sex. He'll take it from his own mother if she gives it up!" My mouth dropped wide open! I looked over at my mother, who looked like she was in deep thought. Then she said in a small, quiet voice, "You can always tell me, I'll believe you because it happened to me."

I wanted to ask her what she meant, but there was a brief, awkward silence and then she snapped back into reality and changed the subject. I was glad he left but I'm sad for my mom that they broke up because of me. I fell asleep thinking of how I would ask my mother what she meant by, "it happened to me." I couldn't wait till the next morning to have that conversation with her. The sun came up and I got up to go to my mother's room. I heard a familiar voice and to my surprise it was Henry and my mother laughing about something. As I walked out of my room I walked into them in their nightclothes. They were acting like nothing had ever happened. He shot a smug look and smiled like he did the night before. This smile said "ha-ha." In return I looked at my mother. I felt like screaming, the feeling of betrayal gripped me so hard that I had to remind myself to breathe. It was a Saturday, so he got dressed and left, and my mother sat me down in the living room to talk. I asked her how she could let him come back. She answered, "I had a long conversation with him, and he knows that that was unacceptable, and it won't happen again!" After that response, I zoned out and I didn't hear another word she said, I only saw her lips moving. I felt so unprotected at that moment!!

Parents reading this, be mindful of how you handle situations of violation when it comes to your children. Most predators will watch to see how far you allow them to go. If you don't put a stop to it, they will continue to violate, moving a step further each time until the ultimate violation happens! I no longer trusted my mother when it came to me after the way she handled the situation. I vowed that from now on I would have to protect and look out for myself.

This would become the norm for us throughout the duration of our time together. Somehow, in my mind, things would happen between us, I would always revert to how she hadn't protected me and didn't choose me and how she never came back for me. I didn't purposely think this way, it just subconsciously happened. The emotional and psychological damage it caused created a barrier between us. I started to build up walls around myself, and anger was festering inside of me. Most of the time I just wanted to yell out what was bothering me, but I never did, I kept it all bottled up inside. Disrespect was not tolerated in our family so most of the time I would suffer in silence. I was incapable of expressing my feelings at the time because I didn't know how to say what I needed to say. Everything was taken as "back talk," even if we were only trying to explain ourselves. The most I got away with was "Man, mama!" when I tried to explain my case, but she definitely would have slapped me, if I went too far. My mother wasn't the type of mother that would hit us on the regular. She would if she needed to, but it wasn't often. That was a result of her getting whooped all the time when she was a little girl. She promised that because of the abuse she endured she wouldn't discipline us through the measures of "beatings." She would let Henry beat the crap out of my brothers and sisters though. He took pleasure in doing it too. Nothing about those beatings was regular discipline. He was a monster and I hated him, and I hated her for letting him touch my siblings…

She had explained how cruel my grandmother was to her growing up and how there was a time she was caught eating mayonnaise out of the jar from the refrigerator. When my grandmother caught her, she made her eat the entire jar of mayonnaise. She said she got sick to her stomach. She didn't have to beat me though because her ways of hurting me became her attitude and her words toward me. I remember vividly one day I was getting ready for school and while standing in the mirror doing my hair, she walked in behind me and said "You think you're cute don't you? Well, you ain't...You are not cute!" I thought what was wrong with her, who says that to their daughter? Where were the positive affirmations, where was the uplifting? I already suffered from low self-esteem and self-worth and when she behaved and said things like this, it made me feel even worse.

Again, generational toxicity is passed down from one jealous mother to the next. I couldn't wait to get on the bus to go to school. I never saw my friends' parents act this way with them. Why was my mother so bitter with me? All this fueled my thoughts that she really didn't like me and that's why she left me. Anyway, I did what I always did, I put on a face, and I went to school. That day was a regular day. I wore my blue dickies uniform pants and white collared shirt, with my white Reebok classics. The lunch bell rang, and my home girl and I couldn't wait to get to the courtyard. We had this friend that we met this year named Lena. Lena was so cool. She loved to laugh and joke. All she did was laugh!! I loved a person whom I could laugh with. The only thing I couldn't figure out was why she wore a full face of makeup every day. I mean she was 14 and she had her brows drawn on, eye makeup, foundation, red lips, and lip liner. That girl was definitely before her time, and she was a really good friend. I just can't tell you what she looked like without the makeup, lol.

Lena walked up and started tripping as usual but this particular day she started to tell me how she was messing around with an older guy. Her: "Girl yeah, older guys are where it's at. They got cars, houses, money, all that!" Me: "What?? Nah, I'm not feeling that I'm scared of older guys." Her: "Whatever! You don't know what ya missing, lol." Lena liked to joke and play a lot, so I had to make sure she wasn't joking this time. Me: This is one of your jokes, right?" Her: "No girl, he's coming to pick me up after school. You will see. I proceeded to ask her how much older the guy was. 16 or 17? She answered and said, "No he's 20!" My mouth dropped open! "Girl, I know you lying, he must want jail time init?" "You better not tell nobody, promise me." "I won't say anything, but you better be careful!" she continued "Besides, sex with older guys is different, you need to get you a boyfriend and try it!" "Girl no way my mother would kill me and I definitely ain't messing with no man, you can count me out!" Until then, nobody had really talked to me about sex. My mother just used to say no boyfriend and don't have sex. I wasn't even sure I knew what sex was. There was no real conversation about it from her although her saying it should be enough because she was my mother and I was supposed to obey her; but it would have helped me if she elaborated on the topic and maybe even explained some of the things that she experienced so that I wouldn't make the same mistakes, but not a single conversation was had.

I put what Lena said to the back of my mind and finished the school day. I didn't think about it again until I got on the bus and saw this guy roll up in a blue Mercedes-Benz with gold rims. Lena came out of the building and jumped into the car with him. As they rode by my bus, I looked out the window. Lena just winked and smiled. I mouthed to her to be careful, and she fanned me off. My bus turned to the left and those gold rims skirted to the right. I couldn't fathom all the things she was experiencing, being 14 with an older guy. Older men who liked younger girls were just creepy to me. I can't explain it, but it was like my subconscious was trying to alert me to certain things. That conversation did spark curiosity about sex though. I thought to myself everyone was doing it or talking about it. In fact, my parents were young when they met and had me. 14 and 16 to be exact. This is what my 14-year-old mind was telling me, and I wanted to talk to someone but who? My parents were unapproachable, and we just didn't have that type of relationship. Life was becoming confusing to me, so many unanswered questions I had. Unfortunately, things at home were not getting better. I couldn't understand why my mother was becoming increasingly distant. She would go into her room and close the door, or she'd leave the house. The adult me realized she was going through so much.

It hurt that we couldn't connect because of all the times I longed to be with her, and I finally got here, but I still felt alone. She was increasing her anger towards me. She argued and fussed and punished me for everything. I wasn't a perfect child but what she was doing was anger displacement. She was angry at Henry's and her life. I started to hear heavy rumors that he was messing around with a young girl at the bottom of the hill. I don't know how true the rumor was, but I know the truth of the situation that happened one day right before my very eyes.

Apparently, my mother and Henry had worked out their differences, AGAIN. It's like no matter what he did she'd always take him back. This time they got engaged to be married. On the day that they had planned to head down to the courthouse my mother got up, did her make-up and her hair, and put on a beautiful navy-blue pants outfit. Her hair was rolled into a French Roll with curls in the front and she rocked pink lipstick on her lips. I thought she looked so pretty. She and I and my Aunt Deanna hopped into her van and drove down the street. I thought we'd be heading toward downtown Jamestown where the courthouse was located. Instead, we stopped in a nearby neighborhood and when she got out of the car, she told me to stay inside.

Through the window, I watched as she banged on one of the apartment doors yelling for Henry to come out. I saw her moving her arms and fists in a fighting motion as she tried to get into the apartment. She came back to the car with tears in her eyes, and none of us spoke during the whole ride home. Come to find out Henry had spent the night before their wedding day at another woman's house. This turned out to be one of the many women he was cheating on my mother with. I felt awful for her, and I couldn't imagine what she was going through at the time. This only caused things to get worse between her and me as she would transfer her anger to me and in return, the rising tension between us contributed to my growing anger issues and rebellion. My father decided that he wanted me to come and live with him. I asked my mother not to send me there. I didn't know him, and I didn't trust him. We had only met a short time before this and the bond or the relationship hadn't grown into a place of trust yet. Especially because his way of dealing with me up until that moment was to turn around and walk away every time he didn't get his way! My mother agreed so we decided that we'd just have to figure it out between her and me. We were all still getting to know each other and still learning this new way of life. I figured it would have been a lot easier than it had been going. You would think that these people would embrace me and love me unconditionally because I was their child but to me, it seemed like I was on trial with my dad. I had to earn his love. There was an imaginary standard level that I must meet before he could treat me the way I should be treated, the way a daughter should be treated by her father.

He didn't give words of affirmation, I never heard my father tell me he thought I was pretty… or beautiful, he never told me he was proud of me for anything. Even as an adult, I'd accomplish many things and he'd never tell me he was proud. Instead, he'd make things about him, and I could feel the feelings of jealousy protruding. He talked about how big my head was and small negative things like that. It sounds funny, but for someone who's already experiencing low self-esteem and who picks themself apart any small negative joke is enough to make them question themselves. I would pick myself apart even more and it took me back to when I was younger, and I stared in the mirror, trying to figure out why my parents abandoned me. I started to blame my appearance like maybe I wasn't pretty enough. Even when he said he loved me, it felt so empty. My mother's non-embracement was more like I love you, but I don't like you. I felt love from her but a strong dislike. This caused me to search myself. I wondered if I had done something as a child that caused this.

All I could remember was my grandmother saying that when I was born my mother didn't like me because life became all about me. She said even my aunts were jealous of me to a certain extent. I thought to myself that my mother couldn't be that shallow or evil, but I remembered that she was just a kid as well. This caused self-hatred in me, like maybe if I weren't born, she would have been happier. Maybe that's why it wasn't hard to leave me behind.

STOP

TO THE YOUNG GIRL, AND EVERY READER READING THIS, I CANCEL EVERY WORD CURSE SPOKEN AGAINST YOU FROM YOUR BIRTH THAT WAS ASSIGNED TO DESTROY YOUR LIFE, YOUR DESTINY, YOUR SELF-WORTH. I COME AGAINST THE FEELINGS OF LOW SELF-WORTH AND INSECURITIES, AND I SAY TO YOU THAT YOU HAVE BEEN FEARFULLY AND WONDERFULLY MADE BY THE HANDS OF THE LORD. GO FORTH AND BE A FORCE TO BE RECKONED WITH ON THE EARTH, ACCOMPLISH EVERY ASSIGNMENT, SLAY EVERY GIANT IN YOUR PATH, AND BE WHO GOD HAS CALLED YOU TO BE! IN THE NAME OF JESUS.

<><><><><><>

All these things caused me to have battles about who I was and who I wasn't. That's when the voice started that told me to kill myself...

One morning I got up to go to school and as I got ready, I went to my mother's bathroom to get toothpaste. While brushing my teeth the voice that had been tormenting me came and spoke loudly in my ear. It said to me, "Do it, kill yourself, get a knife and slit your wrist. She doesn't care about you, and she'll be the first to see your body when she comes out of her room. That will destroy her like she destroyed you!" At that moment, I went to the kitchen, grabbed the knife, and went back into her bathroom. Tears were pouring down my face. I didn't know if I should do this. I didn't want to leave my siblings behind, but I was tired of all the inner torment and pain that I was feeling. I put that knife to my wrist, and I heard another voice say "NO!" I dropped the knife and looked around. This voice was so much louder and stronger than the other voice. I ran and put the knife back and ran out the door to the bus stop. I didn't know it, but that was my first encounter with God! I was so afraid and confused. I went to school that day and suffered my first anxiety attack. I began to hyperventilate, and I slid down the wall of the girl's locker room. I just wanted to die. Some of my classmates ran and yelled for our gym teacher. An ambulance was called, along with my mom. They took my vitals while my class watched. I could see on all their faces that they were really worried. I started to become embarrassed, and I told the paramedics that I was fine and that I just wanted to go to class.

My grandfather showed up at the school to check on me and I told him I was ok and probably was just hungry because I hadn't eaten anything that morning. He hugged me and saw me back to class. I thought about going to the guidance counselor, but what was that gonna do? What was I gonna say? *I'm scared? I tried to kill myself this morning.* In our community that was a huge no-no! People in the African American community didn't talk about depression, suicide, or the fact that they suffered from having thoughts like that. Our people didn't go to counseling. I didn't want CPS to come investigate my mother either. She wasn't a great mom to me, but she didn't deserve that kind of attention, especially with what she had been going through lately with Henry. I mean, she wasn't abusing us. My siblings were happy. *Why would I put my family through any of this?* I decided to keep quiet. I never told anyone until I met my husband years later. I went home like nothing had happened. At this time, I was 14 years old and repeating the eighth grade because I decided to allow my grades to slip my first eighth-grade year and ended up failing my math class. I put in my mind that I was going to get myself together and finish the school year. That night I lay down and commanded the voices in my head to go away and I quickly fell asleep.

STOP

Dear Reader, suicide is not the answer! God is! Suicide will take you straight to an eternity in the fiery pits of hell! There is no repentance after suicide! I silence the voices of Satan and his demons that come to torment you. I cancel the plans of the enemy for your life. I speak life over you, and I bind the works of the enemy against you and your family. I send strength to you to resist the devil, so that he may flee from you!

James 4:7

CHAPTER 9

LOVE IS THAT YOU?

As an adult woman, I often look back and think how foolish we all have been from time to time to think that we were in love with a person at such young ages. In my case, looking for love the way I was looking was very detrimental. The absence of love, the absence of a father, the absence of validation, coupled with a heavy presence of rejection, left girls like me very vulnerable to the streets. Most girls look for love in relationships and sometimes the first male that comes along and expresses that love, whether it's good or bad, is the one into which she will fall. That's what happened to me. As I said before eighth grade, I got so caught up with what was going on in my life that I allowed my math grade to slip down to a 68 by the end of the year. Two points away from a passing grade. I had never failed anything before! Not a major test, not a grade, not a field day race, not anything before this! I had always tried my best to be the best at everything I did. Now I went from being in honors classes to flunking out my last year of middle school. I was disappointed and angry, angry at myself, angry at my family, just angry with my life. All my friends were heading to high school and here I was.… failing. My parents were very upset. They decided that they would not allow me to attend summer school to bring up my grade. My punishment would be the embarrassment of repeating the grade. I thought to myself, *has anyone ever asked if I needed help with homework or needed a tutor?* I wanted to ask these things, but I decided that I needed to take responsibility for my own actions. On top of all that, we were moving. This would make it another new school, uggh. I had been to a different school for every grade of middle school.

Then I thought this might be good. A fresh start and nobody would know I was repeating. My school uniform switched from blue and white to khaki and white. I liked that uniform a lot better. Summer came and went, and the beginning of school approached. This year, my brother and I would attend school together for the first time. He was starting sixth grade and me, well eighth grade again. I remember I started school with two pairs of khaki dickies, three white cotton collared shirts, and a fresh pair of Reebok classics. Without Henry, my mother was now a single mother trying to provide for all of us. This I understood, but I always felt like my needs and wants came last for the simplest fact that my brothers' father paid child support, and Henry took care of the girls well, so he'd stay off child support, but my dad did very little financially for me, as he did emotionally. I remember my mother called my dad's house one evening to speak with him about some information she needed from him to get food stamp benefits for me. His wife answered the phone and told my mom she didn't appreciate her calling at that hour and that she needed to speak to him during normal daytime hours. My mother was livid.

I remember her saying to me "Does your stepmother think I want your father?" We laughed about it, lol. It was nice to laugh with her. After that, she asked me if I would like her to put my dad on child support to help with my needs. I told her no. She replied, "Well, you'll have to go without." I didn't want to do that after the whole foodstamps thing, and I felt like my dad would think I was using him for money. Weird, right? I was trying to be sensitive to the feelings of a man who walked away from my pregnant 14-year-old mother and never looked back. Nevertheless, I just kept pushing and I did what I could with what I had. This is where I learned how to take care of my things. I didn't know when I would be able to get more, so I kept my shoes and clothes clean. I was mindful of what I did throughout the day to not tear or heavily stain my clothing. I washed my white shirts with detergent and bleach, by hand every other day to keep them clean. To this day that was a valuable lesson that stuck with me. I have things in my closet that are well taken care of. Throughout my teenage years, I'd always seem to have a friend who did hair. That meant getting my hair done wasn't an issue, but I had this wavy hair; so even when my hair wasn't done, I slapped water and gel on it and put it into a style called a "fan" or a ponytail. My fan was so long that it hardly just stood straight up. Me and my friends would wear blow pops or ribbons in a bow in front of our fan. I ended up starting school with confidence, despite the huge amount of acne that had begun to trouble my face, sigh.

My homeroom was lit, but our school Techwood Middle School reminded me of "Lean on Me." Our homeroom teacher was also our science teacher, and we gave him a hard time. It seems like they had put a bunch of bad kids in the same class. I met this girl named Shayna, who was troubled and misunderstood. All the things I didn't need to be hooked up with, but everything I needed to be hooked up with! We became close friends. She was funny like me, and all we did was laugh and make jokes in class. There was something mysterious about her though. I guess she could see the same thing about me both coming from not-so-good family lives, but never telling each other exactly what the other was experiencing. It was unspoken, but we could feel each other, that's the thing about connections that are deeper than the surface. It's soul-tied and sometimes soul ties can get you into a lot of trouble. I must say school was going great. I had a solid set of new friends, and I was determined to get my work done this time around. That didn't stop me from being a class clown and getting into trouble though. I'd, heard my dad was a class clown also, like father like daughter, I guess… I would get put out of the class for talking and making jokes. My homeroom teacher, Mr. Saunder, was tired of me; in fact, he was tired of all of us, lol. But every so often I'd catch him laughing and smirking at our jokes.

I walked into the class, sat down, and did what I did every other day, which was waiting for my homegirls, Shayna and Nay, to come in. Nay was a good girl who came from a two-parent home. She was fun and a great friend. The 3 to our 3 amigos. They came in and we started our work. Eventually, some classmates started talking about going to some party. Nay and I were not allowed to go to parties, so we both shook our heads no... Shayna proceeds to tell us how it will be fun, that all the cute boys will be there, and that they would have "that good stuff." "What is good stuff?" I asked, "You know that stuff that gets you high and makes you feel good," she said. "Girl, are you talking about weed? My mother would kill me, no, you can count me out." We both cracked up, at this point. Only we weren't the only ones laughing. There was a boy named Rich, who sat directly behind me in our class. He was super quiet, I mean, almost mute. He was really cute, tall, and light-skinned. Like I said, he hardly ever spoke, so when he cracked a smile to laugh, I caught a glimpse of two gold teeth and one of the cutest smiles I've ever seen. Smiles are my thing... smiles and nice teeth. I played off my surprise as he continued to laugh. I jokingly snapped at him, "Boy what are you laughing at? And why are you all in our conversation?" He responded with a quick, "I'm laughing at you." That small conversation began our friendship. We now had another tripping buddy and eventually, our whole class became a crew.

I've never seen an entire class form such a bond as the one we had. We'd come to school, laugh, joke, copy each other's work, get sent to stand outside the classroom door, and do more things that we shouldn't have been doing; but we also pushed, encouraged, and helped each other. Things were starting to change between Rich and me though. We smiled at each other a little longer and when we would dap up at the beginning of class, he'd hold my hand a little longer. I knew that he liked me, and I think he knew that I liked him too. Everything changed the day we walked into class with the same shoes on. The black low-top Willie Deas had just came out. I had asked my mother if she could get me another pair of shoes because even though I was cleaning my shoes and polishing them with white shoe polish, wearing one pair of white shoes every day was not going to work. She called my grandfather, Charles, and he gave her some money for the sneakers. When we both walked in with them on, of course Shayna and our other classmate, Dub, started "cooing" and saying, "Look at the twins." "Oh, please," I replied, "it's not even like that." To my surprise, Rich said, "It could be like that if you want it to be, I mean you could be my girl."

I looked at him, thinking he was joking but he wasn't laughing. He seemed a bit nervous. I was completely caught off guard by the whole situation. I mean I had liked other boys before and talked to boys on the phone and even called them my boyfriend, like Tre, but never had a real boyfriend. Rich was looking at me, waiting for my response. "Yeah, I could be your girl," was all I could think of saying! He asked for my number and said he'd call me that night. This would be the beginning of what I thought was forever. I was never the kind of girl who wanted to be with a whole bunch of different guys, and in my opinion, most girls wanted that one true love that would last forever. Nobody sits and thinks to themselves, "Yeah, I just wanna go out and sleep around with a bunch of different guys," but most of us are misguided. A lot of us didn't have fathers to teach us how little boys think and what they are truly after. A father's love, guidance, and presence in a daughter's life is what she needs to be able to know when a guy is running a game on her. A father's love is supposed to show a daughter what real love looks like so they can identify it in a mate. When it is absent a girl doesn't know how to recognize if a guy is just around to please himself and is not really there to care for her heart. In my case, my father was the first man to break my heart so what I received from him is what I attracted to myself. Broken promises, dismissal, and heartache. I fell hard into what older folks were calling, "Puppy Love." I started thinking the world of this guy and in my eyes, he could do no wrong. Puppy Love should be renamed Fake Love because I found out that I was not real…

The conversation between him and me was sweet and he actually seemed to care. I became addicted to the "how's your day?" and the "what's up with you?" This is what I considered my very first real relationship. People at school knew we were boyfriend and girlfriend, and nobody was running up to me with stories about him cheating. I was even surprised when my mother, who had always given me the third degree about everything, especially boys, allowed me to see him. I got to hang out at his house and go on my first fair date with him, his mom, and his sisters. His mother seemed to like me and allowed me to visit all the time, she even picked me up. I became close friends with his sisters. This was different for me. It felt good. I didn't think that I was only 14 and too young to be "in love." I wanted the opposite of what I was seeing my mother do. She and Henry were over completely, but she had started to have other male friends. In our community what my mother was doing was normal, most people's mothers had "friends." I never judged her for it, I just knew I wanted something different. The knowledge of different men visiting my mother's house psychologically damaged me. I felt dirty when her "friends" came over. I never heard or saw her be inappropriate with them, I would just see them come and go. I don't believe she was engaging in sexual activities when all of them, but she kept each one around to serve whatever purpose they served.

Seeing my mom's experiences encouraged me to decide at an early age that I wanted something different. That didn't make me better than her, and that's not a slight to her. That's what growth is supposed to look like. I hope my children learn from my mistakes and do better than I did! My mother had had a very difficult childhood, which contributed to who she was and the decisions she made that ultimately caused her to lose her life…

In Rich, I had found love. He was funny, handsome and all about me or so it seemed, and as you might expect, he ended up telling me that he loved me. When you are rejected and deprived of love as a child, especially by your parents, you tend to look for it in all the wrong places. Those three words put together in a sentence can be very dangerous. It turned out to be the most dangerous phrase of my life. We had been going together now for months. The Fair, Thanksgiving, and Christmas had passed. Then it came, the first "I love you" and the pause after waiting on my response. I said, "I love you, too." Who cares if I was only in the eighth grade? I thought we were truly in love. The fairytale love….that's what it seemed like was happening to me. We would be this way for months and everything was good. We never really discussed the topic of being intimately involved. This is what led me to believe he wasn't after it because it wasn't the focus of our relationship. But eventually, that day came...

I was hanging out around his way with a few of my homegirls, and I paged him to tell him we were about to walk down the street. By the time I hung up my friend's phone he had pulled up on his bike. We all laughed at how fast he got there. We stood outside and chopped it up with the crew for a minute, but what began as a group hangout quickly turned into us dismissing them and slowly heading toward his house. "You want to ride my bike? I'll walk?" he asked. "No thanks, I'll walk. Lol," I answered. "You should get on the handlebar," he said. "H*** no, so you could drop me off the bike. No, I'll walk." We laughed and walked slowly. "Do you want to go to my house?" He asked. "Yeah, I wanna say hello to your mother." He told me his mother was not at home and that no one was there.   I got butterflies in my stomach, but I couldn't let him know that. I was tough, *what was I gonna say? No, I'm scared to go to your house?* Maybe I should have, but I didn't. Instead, I said "Yeah I'll go." This was the first time we had ever been alone, and I was nervous. We sat down on the couch like usual and turned on the TV. I can handle myself, I'm in control of the situation. Nothing is going to happen...

PAUSE:

Dear young reader, I highly suggest that when dating or courting someone you and that person do not spend time alone in intimate spaces. Even though I wasn't saved at the time, I wish someone had shared this advice with me, then I would have at least had a voice of reason speaking to me in the back of my mind advising me against these things. When you're alone, temptations will come, and before you know it you have moved from point A to point B, and point B is hard not to revisit once you've been there.

That evening we graduated from point A to point B and it happened so quickly. One minute we were sitting on the couch and the next we were holding hands and exchanging kisses. His bedroom was close to the living room and before I knew it, we had gotten up and the door closed behind us. The car ride home that night didn't feel the way I thought it would, although I was quiet and inside myself, I didn't feel bad or ashamed. I thought I would although I did ask myself 1 million questions like *why would you do that? Was this the right time? Was he the right one?* I didn't feel ashamed though. Maybe if I had it would've caused me to stop and I may never have gotten my heart broken, but honestly it wouldn't have mattered. I had already been yoked to him with my heart and my mind way before my body. It seemed right because he was the only one who had loved me or shown me any type of love. I was blinded by what I thought love was, but in reality, I didn't know what it looked like. So now I went home and dreamed about marriage, love, and children. I felt like a grown woman when I was a misguided girl who should've never been feeling these feelings in the first place. Now I crave to hear those words from him, and a nature has been awakened in me that desires to fulfill its lust. The need to feel loved and accepted was about to take me on a further emotional roller coaster, and I wouldn't have anyone to help me out of the mess that I got myself into.

STOP:

Fornication is sexual intercourse between people who are not married. The Bible calls to every man, woman, young, and old when it says in 1 Corinthians 6:18 "Flee sexual immorality, every sin that a man does is outside of the body, but he who commits sexual immorality sins against his own body. 2 Timothy 2:22 also calls for us to "flee, youthful lust, but pursue righteousness, faith, love, peace with those who call on the Lord out of a pure heart." God designed sex for marriage, and for marriage to be a holy and honored institution and covenant. The Bible calls for husbands and wives to keep themselves exclusively for one another or face God's judgment. Those who persistently indulge in fornication will not inherit the kingdom of God. If you are indulging in sexual immorality, fornication, adultery, homosexuality, lesbianism, or pornography, this is your time to repent. Ask God for forgiveness and turn from your sins. Make a conscious decision to stop indulging and ask God to deliver you, wash you clean, and make you whole in every area of your life. God loves you and wishes that no man, woman, boy, or girl would perish, but remember the wages of sin is death, which is eternal separation from God, but the gift of God is eternal life with him.

Puppy love is defined as intense but relatively shallow, romantic attachment associated with adolescence. The adolescent mind is a very delicate frame or space. It is young, immature, and inexperienced. It needs guidance and help to make good decisions. It lacks emotional intelligence, mental maturity, and social skills, which leads to poor decision-making and impulse behavior. This is the main reason my husband and I decided not to allow any of our children to date during the period that they were in school. After our daughter graduated high school and cosmetology school and she was still living at home, she began dating a young man, and we were able to help guide her through her decision-making since she had never dated before. Waiting to date or court leaves space for the immature mind to grow into maturity, and it also eliminates unnecessary heartbreak and stress… WAIT until you have the mental maturity and have learned to love yourself and God before you decide to date.

CHAPTER 10

RUN

Things change when you become sexually active. It's like my eyes became open like Adam and Eve when they partook of the forbidden fruit of the Tree of Knowledge of good and evil. I felt different, and I spent most of my days warring with myself about whether or not what I was doing was right. Either way, I kept doing it and there was no turning back. What I didn't know was I could stop and that I didn't have to keep doing it. It didn't help that influences around me were doing it. Society made it seem like it was ok. Even the pastors never preached about it. I didn't have many healthy marriages around me either. Before you knew it, me and my friends were either sneaking out or sneaking our boyfriends in. That was heavily prevalent where I was from. On Mondays, the bathroom is where all the girls dished their "tea" of what they were doing over the weekend. Not me though, I was still shy and kept a tight lip about what I was doing. I didn't think it was any of their business anyway. Meanwhile, at home, my mom and I were still having our difficulties. Sometimes she would be so happy with me. I loved her good mood days!

Like the times when her friends came over and she would ask me to sing "The Song" for them. I remember it was the same song every time, Deborah Cox's "Nobody's Supposed To Be Here." It was a song about love and heartbreak. They'd sing along, rock in their seats, snap their fingers, and drink what was in their cups like we were in an R&B club. Everyone would clap and scream when I belted out the famous line "nobody no no no no no no no no no no nooooooooooo." I held that note and finished the song, Mama would say thank you, and I went back to my room. I never realized I could sing until then, but music was always an outlet for me.

Then there were the bad days, like the day I ran away from home… to this present day, I don't recall what it was that we were disagreeing about. All I know is I went to school with a huge attitude and when I got there, I decided I didn't want to be there. I never cut school before, but that would be the day. I looked at Shayna and she looked at me… "If we gonna go, we need to go before we get inside. It'll be harder to leave then," she said. "Let's roll," was my response and we left. It was like I was slowly starting not to care about anything anymore. I didn't have a plan at all… I mean, the plan was to just skip school and make it home by the time I was supposed to be home, but as the day went on those plans changed. Shayna and I walked and laughed and laughed some more. This was what I loved about her. She could see the funny side of any situation. She laughed at the thought of my mother rolling up in her van as we were ducking and dodging through the neighborhood. "Boy, big Denise going to hit you with a two-piece and throw your *bleep *bleep in the car!"

"Yeah, your mama gonna knock your head off with that stick she got behind the door, lol." Why we thought it was funny I have no idea, but we were falling down, laughing along the sidewalk. I can honestly say that I've never had a friend like her. We finally got to the hangout spot where some of the other kids go when they cut school. There was nothing to do really but hang out. I figured I just needed a mental break!

All of a sudden somebody passed a blunt around and to my surprise when it got to Shayna, she puffed and passed it like it was second nature. I tried to hide my face. Then somebody passed it to me. "I'm good," I said. "What's up with you Shawty? You got to hit this if you want to hang out on this block." Before I could answer, Rich pulled up on his bike and said, "No, she said she's good." "Let's go y'all two," he said as he pointed to me and Shayna. We walked off laughing. Shayna teased him "Boy, Rich who you think you is? I guess you run things around here talking about some let's go y'all two." Lol, this man thinks he got us in check, huh?" She continued through her laughter. "Girl, are you high?" I asked. "Matter of fact, never mind sit right here on the curb so you can come down. Rich asked me what I was about to do, to which I replied, "Nothing just hang out." He shot me that smile and his gold teeth beamed. "I gotta run a short errand. I'm gonna come back for y'all." I found myself thinking, *what kind of errand?* It didn't dawn on me that my boyfriend was doing something he had no business doing. I found out later that he found himself a hustle and it wasn't cutting grass. I would never see him smoke or hustle, but when 2+2 comes together and makes 4 the answer is definitely 4. The day was going by quickly and before we knew it, we had hung out on the block all day. The school buses rolled through and by the time Rich's sister was walking through the gate of their yard, we had made our way to the outside of the gate as well, "What's up Dani, what are you doing around here?" she asked. "I skipped school today." Oh ok, cool she said as she headed into the house. Rich pulled back up on his bike and asked if we were hungry. We decided to walk to the Burger Hunt which was like a two-minute walk from his house. After we ate, there was nothing to do but go home.

Right around the time we finished eating, my pager started going off. It was my mom. I was still mad at her. Come to think of it, I was mad beyond what had happened this morning. My anger stretched back to the day she left me to rot at my grandparents' house, so I made the decision not to answer my beeps. I didn't think she cared about me my entire life, so I didn't see the point of why she was blowing up my pager. It was also at that moment I decided not to go home. I know I ran out but there was no turning back now. I turned to Shayna to tell her I thought I wasn't going to go home. At first, she looked at me to see if I was serious. I think she knew that for me, this was overboard and out of character; nevertheless, she was down to spending the night out. I hadn't thought past this point. I didn't know where we were going or how we were going to get there. Rich asked if we wanted him to walk us to my house and I told him I wasn't going home but didn't know where I was going. I got a spot y'all can chill at, my homeboy and his people are out of town, and they let us use their spot if we need it. I asked if he was sure they wouldn't mind, and he said we would be good. We headed out on foot, and he was on a bike. The more we walked, the closer we got to my neighborhood. That's when I asked him where we were going. "I'm taking you home," he said. "No way, I'll turn around right now," I said. He said he was joking, although he did think I should go home.

I started to think I should too. I mean I know my mother was gonna be upset, but maybe I wouldn't get into so much trouble if I went home now. That little devil on my left shoulder still said not to go home, and unfortunately, that was the voice of influence in my ears these days. As we approached my street I started sweating. Rich must have felt my nervousness because he looked over and laughed. "My homeboy's house is next door to yours." *Is this a joke?* I wondered. *Why would I want to run away and sleep next door to my house?* He thought that we'd be safe closer to home, and he was right. We ducked off down the side street so we wouldn't walk directly past my house. I glanced over toward my house and saw my mom's car outside. The light from inside shined through the window. The outside was dark, and the house looked sad. I could feel my mother's worry. I felt her wondering, *where is my child?* Right then I should've gone home and taken whatever punishment I had coming to me, but I was so angry, emotional, and confused at the time. It's like I wanted her to know my heart and feel my pain and know what it felt like to be left and not know if the person you were waiting to see walk through the door was going to ever come back. That thought drove me to keep walking. We made it to the friend's house. He opened the door, and we went inside. He hung out for a while and then he rode off on that bike. "See y'all tomorrow." He said, "All right see you tomorrow." I got situated to go to sleep on the couch but before I fell asleep, I looked out of the window and caught a glimpse of my mother's room window, just as she cut her light off. A feeling of sadness shook me, and I shook it off. My mom and brothers and sisters were nervous and afraid that something bad had happened to me and I didn't even care because I was trying to punish my parents for what they had done to me. *Who was I becoming? Why had I allowed Anger to take over and lead my life?*

A little while on the couch and I was asleep. The next morning, we got up and I decided to take a shower. I always kept extra clothes in my book bag because I had gym and my mom always taught me to carry a care bag with extra underwear, pads, deodorant, etc. just in case my cycle came on at school or had an emergency. As I walked down the hall, I saw bags of clothes, and the rooms appeared to be packed up. I didn't question it until I got to the bathroom, turned the knob to the shower, and found out that there was no water. By now I'm thinking it started to look like nobody lives here or maybe these people were in the process of moving. Fear kicked in now because my mind was telling me that maybe these people didn't know Rich and his homies were using this place or maybe they could, but we weren't supposed to be there. So, it was time to roll. I peeked out the windows and saw that my mom's car was gone. As I grabbed my book bag, I picked up the phone to call Rich. He answered on the first ring, and for some reason, I could hear him, but he couldn't hear me. The phone was full of static and fuzzing in and out. I called back five times with no success. Something didn't feel right. I grabbed Shayna and we headed out the door. It was Friday so people would see us in our uniform and think we were walking to school. The plan was to make it to Rich's house and shower and figure out my next move.

Just as we hit the top of the road, I saw Rich's mom's car and my mom's car zip off the side road. I grabbed Shayna by the shirt collar and pulled her into the corner store. It happened to be some type of Japanese place, so I was yelling, asking the lady where the back door was. "Maam, where is the back door?" All she did was look at us like we were crazy and spoke something in Japanese. I wasn't sure my mother had seen us so we might be ok, but who was I kidding, of course she saw me. She was LOOKING for me! Apparently, she wasn't the only one. When my mother pulled up, the police pulled up too. They came into the store and caught us hiding in an aisle. "Put your hands up girls. Both of you." Shayna and I were handcuffed and put into the back of the police car. I couldn't believe it. This lady had called the cops on me. I had always heard the boys on the block say we don't talk to the police and here my own mama had called them. I was even more angry! Like so angry that it didn't dawn on me that I was about to go to DJJ. As I grew even madder, I looked out the window and my mother was talking to the police but looking right at me. First, she had a disappointed look that quickly turned to anger. I couldn't concentrate too much because, at the time, Shayna was fidgeting like crazy.

"Girl, What are you doing, keep still?! Are you trying to get the cuffs off?!" "No fool, look!" she said. I looked at this girl as she pulled a baggie of weed out of her pocket and shoved it inside the seat. Now I'm scared. *Was she crazy? What if they found that? We are both going to jail!* "Just be quiet anybody could've put that there." Now I'm really scared. Just then the officer swung open my door, pulled me out of the car, and said, "Dani, we are releasing you to your mother." I was relieved to have the cuffs off, but I looked at Shayna through the window. "Wait I'm not leaving my friend." "She is going to call her parents and we're going to take her home." I didn't believe him at all. My mother wasn't a stranger to the game, so she quietly said to me, "We'll wait right here until Shayna talks to her mom." The female officer went over and asked her for her mother's number. I heard her talking to her mom and I felt a little better, but I still couldn't help but wonder why they just couldn't release her to my mother, so we could take her home. Either way, I wasn't looking forward to any of this day. The police didn't let me speak to Shayna, so she never heard me say that I didn't want to leave her and that we made sure she talked to her mom. All she knew was that I was uncuffed standing with my mother and the police were driving her off, cuffed in the back seat. She shot me a cold look as the cop car pulled out into traffic.

The police car was still in eye view when my mom and Rich's mom started in on me. "What the h*** were you thinking, Dani? You got your mama and all of us worried about you. You could've been killed, kidnapped, raped, drugged, or in a ditch somewhere. Ms. Adrian was going off and I couldn't even think of the words to describe how dumb I felt. As soon as she finished. My mom looked at me and said, "Let's go." When we got in the car it was like somebody sounded an alarm as she went off. She went on and on and on about how she told Rich if he really cared for me, he'd tell them where I was and that's how she found out I had stayed in an abandoned house next door. *Abandoned??* Now it all made sense. The bags, the packed rooms, the water off, the phone… and Rich the snitch. I was so mad at him for telling and I couldn't wait to see him on Monday and not for the usual reasons either. We pulled up to the house and I was immediately met by a house full of people. My mother had kept my siblings home from school and my cousins, who were my Aunt Deanna's boys, were there. I walked past them, went to my room, grabbed my clothes, and jumped into the shower. I didn't want to see or hear from anybody. As I left the bathroom, my mom yelled for me to come to her room. "Give me your beeper. I'm turning it off" she said. "Why?" I asked. "Why??? Because there's no need for you to have it since you weren't answering any of my pages." Now in my head, I was thinking, *why would I answer if I ran away; besides Granddaddy Charles bought me this pager and he pays the bill.* I didn't say it out loud, but I might as well have because I wasn't ready for what happened next. "Dani pull your pants down and lay across my bed." "Huh, Mama what are you talking about?" "Dani, I'm not gonna tell you again…keep your underwear up, but pull down your pants, now!"

I looked at her like she was crazy. My mother had never whooped me before. She slapped my glasses off for talking back to her once. She had made me clean my sisters' room, which was a disaster. I mumbled, "These are not my kids, but I always gotta watch them and clean up after them and I never get to go outside anymore." She was standing in the hallway and before I knew it, she ran into the room and slapped me so hard, my glasses flew behind the bed! One other time she chopped me with a plastic bat for something, but she never spanked me or gave me a beating; so, what she was doing now was foreign. Initially, I thought about running again, but this time she probably would have fought me; so eventually, I pulled down my pants and lay across the bed. She pulled out a thick leather belt and began to chop me over and over again. Between every chop, she paused to say something. "I'm doing this because I love you, Dani, don't you ever run away from me again, I'm your mother and I love you!" I could hear tears welling up in her throat as she yelled at me. "This hurts me more than it hurts you!" I buried my face into her bed and screamed and then the longer the beating lasted, I just lay there on the side of my face and whimpered. It seemed like forever, but when she finally stopped, I pulled up my pants and ran out of her room. My brothers and cousins were laughing uncontrollably as I ran past them.

I slammed the door of the room that I shared with my two sisters. I ran my hands over my butt and legs and felt the stinging welts. I became even more enraged. Suddenly I thought back to the beating, and what she was saying. *Wait a minute, did my mother just tell me that she loved me?* Until that point, I don't recall her ever saying "I love you" to me. I heard her say "I love my kids" or "I love y'all, we all we got," but I never heard her say "I love you, Dani." A fluster of emotions came over me, and as quickly as I had been upset, I became overwhelmed with another emotion. It was a mixture of happiness because it seemed like she was accepting me, and sadness that it came during a beating. Sadly, I wasn't crying anymore because of the beating. I was crying because I finally felt like my mother cared about me like she did my other siblings, but it came out at the time of discipline. *What does this mean???* I cried and cried and cried… the next thing I knew I had fallen asleep.

CHAPTER 11

LOVE IS BLIND

I woke up the next morning and decided that I wasn't going to get out of bed… or so I thought. Mama came into my room yelling to get up and clean the house. She told me I was not allowed to use the phone, go outside, or have company. Blah blah blah blah blah. After a while, what she would be saying was going into one ear and out the other. My thoughts drifted to Shayna, then to Rich, then to school. I was wondering if my classmates were going to somehow know what happened. I wondered what had happened to Shayna, and what Rich was going to think when he found out I was under punishment. Not only was I restricted from phone privileges, but also when I got them back, I would only be allowed to use it on the weekends, but only half a day on Sundays. That weekend rolled by in a blur, and I nervously anticipated school on Monday. It came though, and I had no other choice but to face it. I got to school and to my surprise everyone acted the same, except Dub. When I came in, he smiled and said, "I know y'all cut school!" We laughed and I found my seat and waited for Rich to come to class. He came in first with a nervous look on his face. "Yo, what happened?" He asked. "I got in trouble, and she put me on punishment." That's all I could get out before I turned my head and saw Shayna walk into the classroom just before the bell rang. I looked at her and she looked away quickly and didn't say a word.

The entire day went by, and Shayna and I didn't speak, which was unusual, because we had all the same classes. At lunch, I finally caught up to her as she tried to completely ignore me. "Hey Shayna," I said. At first, she didn't say anything! "Hey Dani, what's up?" "Nothing but it seems like you're avoiding me. Are you OK? Did you get into trouble?" She hesitated for a bit and then said, "Dani everything's all right I just don't wanna talk about it." I went on to ask if she wanted to eat lunch and she told me no, she was just going to eat with Sasha, who was another girl in our class. I said ok, but it really wasn't ok with me. Still, I figured I needed to let her have her space. I had other problems to worry about anyway. One was how I was going to maintain a relationship without my privileges and two was the fact that my parents were on my case. My father was furious, and he and my mother weren't seeing eye to eye. He wanted to "co-parent" me but didn't think he could do that from his house with me living with my mom. He was upset with my mother also because this was around the time that she found out that I wasn't a virgin anymore and she decided to put me on birth control.

He came over to our house and he and my mother argued. He got so mad that he started beating on my mother's table with his fist. "Why would you put her on birth control without telling me or talking to me about it?" "Because you don't have to worry about raising a baby if she gets pregnant!" "Then I want her to come and live with me!" "Well, Dani doesn't want to come live with you!" "See that's the problem Denise, why is she allowed to make decisions? She's a child and putting her on birth control gives her a pass to have sex!" "Well Ron, I'm sorry but I'd rather let her be on birth control than to be pregnant. Remember what happened between me and you!" I started to realize how serious everything was getting. *Pregnant??* I wasn't trying to have a baby!! I thought to myself that couldn't happen because I've never had unprotected sex. Either way, my dad turns to me and says, "Dani, I can't do this like this. You are here with your mom, and I can't raise you outside of my house; so right now, I need to focus on the kids at my house, the kids that live with me." After that, he left, and I felt the same feelings that I felt as a small girl. *Why does he leave? He always seems to abandon me, to turn his back on me. All because I don't live up to his standards and expectations, he was always looking down his nose at me.*

I felt sick to my stomach and ran to my room. I felt like I was never going to be good enough and I'd never be able to earn his love. Yes, I had made some terrible choices, but my bad choices stemmed from somewhere. Instead of someone helping me, everyone just turned their backs and functioned as if their actions didn't fuel my behavior. My daddy never showed me love, just a whole lot of criticism and neglect. Now wasn't the time to walk away. Now was when I needed the guidance, but because it wasn't his way on his terms, he did what he'd done before and what he'd do again. He had a temper tantrum and stormed off. I continued to build up walls around me, brick by brick, blocking people out and barricading myself in. My mother walked in and said softly, "your dad was wrong for telling you that he must focus on the kids at his house as if you're not worth his time. He's just upset, he'll come around." That's just it, he stopped coming around and it would be a long time before I would see him again. This made me run to Rich even more. The love I was searching for I could get from him, or so I thought.

My next disappointment was headed my way fast and I was too blind to see it coming. Time went on, and the cute puppy love stage wore off. During the times of my punishment, Rich would sneak to my house, and I'd let him in when my mother went to sleep. We weren't always doing something inappropriate. Sometimes he just came over and went to sleep, I figured I must really be special if he just wanted to be near me. Boy, was I naive. One night my brother Juice snuck out and attempted to 'steal" my mother's car. He was probably about 9 or 10 years old. He ended up driving the car into the ditch. This was one of the nights Rich was on his way to my house. Juice was outside trying to figure out how to get the car out of the ditch. When I looked out the window Juice was in the driver's seat, and Rich was pushing the car out of the ditch. Juice never told me that Rich was sneaking in, and I never told him that he was taking Mama's car.

Rich and I would date for a year, and he would continue to sneak over and be up and gone by daylight. This would go on even more after we moved to the G-Road Westside. It was so much easier there because this house had the back door inside my room. My mind was blown. I would've never thought my mother would give me that room. I think, at this point, she was doing her own thing and not caring about what I was doing. She had a new friend named Ike and Henry was still around since he was my sister's father. My mother was not paying me any attention. I almost thought it was a setup. Also, by this time, Shayna and I had stopped being friends. I think she never forgave me for what went down that day. She left school and to this day I've never seen her again. Losing that friendship was another letdown for me.

I was starting to think it was me! In those times my self-esteem was non-existent. I just hated everything about myself. I was overly critical of myself, and I felt that those around me were overly critical of me too. Losing Shayna as a friend took me back to when I was younger, and I stood in the mirror and picked myself apart to find a reason I was being rejected. I did what I always did though which was to suck it up and I kept it pushing. Rich had a sister my age and a sister younger than me. Hanging out with them made it a little bit easier to get over losing Shayna.

I started hanging out with them more and more. We became friends and I even started to feel like a part of their family, only I wasn't. Even though we were close, and they were cool. I wasn't a part of their family. My parents never knew how abandonment and rejection left me vulnerable to so many things and so many people. It caused me to want to be accepted by someone… anyone… it left me trying to fit in with other people and be a part of other people's families. It sounds pretty lame, right? I wasn't even doing it on purpose. It was just what my brain was doing to try to find me love. I guess the love that I thought I had found was not true love, after all. I was at Rich's house one day, talking to his sisters, and the younger sister said, "I've got something to tell you." As I waited for her to tell me I watched as her eyes looked at her older sister for a response. The older sister looked away from her with an "I don't want anything to do with this" type of look. The younger sister continued after I begged her to tell me. "This isn't easy for me to say Dani so I'm just gonna say it. Rich has been cheating on you with Taylor, and he even bought her a pair of sneakers." All kinds of things were going through my mind. For one, this whole thing seemed like a joke. I played cool in front of the sisters, but when I got home, I went to my room and cried my eyes out. When my mother came in and asked me what was wrong. I refused to answer. Instead of her leaving it alone, she called Rich's house and asked his sister and I'm guessing they told her what happened.

I was mad at her because I didn't want them to know that I was crying. I just wanted to be left alone. I don't remember my mother consoling me at all. We just argued, and I wanted her to mind her business. I didn't want to talk about the extreme heartbreak I was experiencing. I didn't want to hear her say this is why you shouldn't be in a relationship. Maybe I should have allowed her that space to comfort me, she had had her share of heartbreak so maybe she did understand. I had watched her go through abuse with Henry and she kept taking him back, so what was she going to tell me at that moment? I shut down and decided that I needed to power up to deal with Rich. I called him and began yelling at him. "How are you gonna be cheating on me with Taylor?? She's in the sixth grade and she's messing around with all the boys. Are you crazy? I'm done with you!" I didn't even let him say anything. I hung up the phone and immediately after, I felt like crap. I wanted to cry, kick, and scream; instead, I did what I always did. I sucked it up and kept moving! These things that were happening to me were making my exterior harder and harder. A few days went by and on that third night, I heard a "tap tap" on my door. I know good and well this guy is not knocking on my door. I yanked the door open and said with an attitude, "What!!??"

He looked at me with the grin that I always thought was so cute, but now it just looked dumb. "I guess you're still mad. Do you think I can come in? You didn't give me a chance to say anything." Against my better judgment, I let him in. See ladies, that's the compromising, unhealed part of us that deeply wants the truth to be a lie. All we need to hear him say is "I didn't do it," and we will take him back. This is what happened that night. I opened my ears to hear a lie and closed my eyes so I wouldn't see the truth. I became "blinded by love." I let a creep, creep back into my heart that night, and I would pay for it with my heart as well. Once a male sees that you will allow anything and that you don't have the spiritual or authoritative figure of a father or older male figure, he will devour you until you get fed up… IF you get fed up! Rich and I never made it official that the breakup was off. I would have felt a little dumb if I had to tell his sisters that I took him back, so we just kept it the way it was.

Secretly sneaking into my house every night just to sleep in my twin-size bed. Something in my heart had changed though. He got put into the category with my father, my mother, and even Henry. I didn't trust him anymore. I loved him a little less and a little less. The lyrics to Avant's song separated, rang in my head. "Every time I see you, I get a bad vibe… mmmhmm hmm… when we were together, we never turned our backs on each other but now that we're separated, we can't stand one another."

I decided that I would control how this went. Yeah, I'm in control! I convinced myself that the intercourse was for me. When actually my 14/15-year-old body got no pleasure or enjoyment. I was fooling myself in a big way. This went on for some months, the battle between lust and emotions, my mind, and my heart. Until one day I went over to Rich's house to hang out with his sisters. No one knew that we were still boyfriend and girlfriend, so we acted like we were just friends to everyone else. I walked in and said what's up, he did the same and left. The sisters and I did what we normally did. We conversed about what was new and one of them said, " Girl, did Rich tell you he got a baby on the way?" I almost passed out! I tried to play cool…and said "No, why would he tell me that?" "I mean I know y'all were cool and all after y'all broke up." she finished. "No, we don't talk about stuff anymore just cordial, so is it with Taylor?" "No, this girl from down the street who he was talking to…" I started doing all kinds of math in my head. We had not too long ago, broken up, so I figured he was messing with us both, and Lord knows who else at the same time. I became infuriated. I didn't show any emotion. I just couldn't wait to see him that night. As usual, the "tap tap" at the door came. I opened it and I let it pour!!! I cursed him out! I was so mad I didn't even care. I told him to get his dumb so and so out of my house and never to come back… EVER again. He didn't say a word… not

I'm sorry… not anything. I watched him walk out of my yard and another part of my heart shattered. I stood in the doorway….broken.

"Love is blind, and it will take over your mind. What you think is love is truly not, you need to elevate and find"- EVE , rapper.

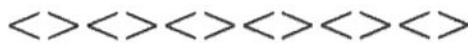

PAUSE:

Having traumatic experiences in childhood, such as abandonment, neglect, and rejection may invite in the struggle of low self-esteem and self-worth. This can cause you to settle for unhealthy relationships and you may feel that you don't deserve better. My self-worth and esteem as a child were very low. I figured that I must not be worth anything because my parents didn't love or want me. This caused me to look for love in all the wrong places and for emotional attachments to people who didn't have my best interest at heart. The sting of abandonment would send me into shock each time these people exited my life. What I needed to know was that although I was not loved or chosen by my family, I was already loved and chosen before birth by God!

Dear Reader, if you're reading this, don't allow the struggle of seeking to be loved, validated, and chosen to cause you to settle for unhealthy relationships. You are valuable, you are loved, and you were chosen by God, and when the time is right, He will send you a mate who will love you, care for you, and look after your heart.

CHAPTER 12

DÉJÀ VU

From this point, life began to drag on. Although I was on top of my grades, my behavior started to decline. As an adult, I now advise other parents to pay attention to their children's behavior, because if they start showing signs of acting out, often it's a cry for attention or some sort of trouble. I was experiencing my first heartbreak from a relationship, and I was confused. I couldn't talk to anyone about it, and I think not having an outlet was crushing as well. If only I had a mentor of some sort! Maybe I could talk to my guidance counselor; but then, too much would leave my lips and my family would be upset with me, so I directed my anger into other areas of my life like fighting. I wasn't a bully, nor did I start fights. In fact, every fight that I was in was usually because of someone else, but it became a way to let my aggression out. I wish someone had taught me how to channel that energy into something positive or even thrown me into a boxing ring and taught me how to professionally fight and control my emotions. My friends and I did a lot of street fighting. Being violent was easy at first because I had a lot of built-up animosities, and although all the altercations were a result of being picked on, I still felt bad afterward. This was not something that I wanted to be doing and most of these battles were due to who I was hanging around with and the beef they were having.

The fights I can remember were because my friend was being picked on and you know if one fights all fight. I was "ride or die" and my people knew that. So, we ended up fighting at school and got put up for expulsion. By the power of God, the board decided to let us stay at school and not expel us and I vowed to stop all getting in trouble and focus on graduating. Rich had stopped going to school, so he wasn't a distraction. Thank God! The expulsion scare was enough to set me on the right track and I ended up graduating. I was so happy to be leaving all this middle school drama behind. I figured I could have another fresh start at a new school with new people and a new perspective. After Shayna had left, I became close friends with a girl named Desiree. In fact, Desiree was the reason I was always in beefs or fights, lol. Girls would always pick on her. I think it had to do with jealousy. Anyway, Desiree and I started making plans for our freshman year. I had passed, but she had failed so she had to go to summer school. She pushed through and passed. We were very excited because we had the whole summer to hang out and plan our outfits for ninth grade. We were going to a school without uniforms.

I had worn uniforms since the seventh grade. Where we lived was zoned for a school called L.B. Warrior High School. I couldn't wait to get there! Summer was rolling by and when Desi and I weren't hanging out I hung out with my boy-crazy cousin, Alicia. We were the same age but her track-record with the fellas was extensively long. She loved to dress cute, and she always had her own money because she braided hair. She stayed in drama and fights. Nevertheless, she was my family and I loved her. What I didn't like was how she always wanted to hook me up with someone, usually the cousin of whoever she was talking to at the time. After the situation with Rich, I had told myself that I would chill for a minute. I didn't want to think about boys! I was starting to see that they were no good just like my dad, Henry, and all the other guys my mom had been dealing with. I was still fresh off the breakup, and I didn't ever want to feel that again. The only way to not feel that again was to not get another boyfriend. I expressed all this to Alicia and her response to me was "That's the wrong way to think about it. Moving on is the way to get over your ex; besides, you need to loosen up, you're too stuck up." I wanted to say, "so you want me to have whore-ish tendencies." But I rephrased and just told her, "No, I'm good!"

At this time, she was dating a guy named Black and of course, he had a cousin who was around our age and Alicia thought he'd be perfect for me. "You don't gotta take it serious, just something for the summer…come on this will be fun… blah blah blah" I gave in and told her yes after she kept whining and begging. This would be the beginning of me being set up with my friends' boyfriends, friends/ brothers/ cousins. I should have just said no. I headed over to Alicia's grandmother's house the following weekend to hang out with her and Black and to meet the cousin. When I got there, she braided my hair and told me to change my shirt and shoes. She gave me her green hi-top Reeboks with the straps and her lime green jersey. I kept my Capri pants on. "Girl was what I had on not good enough?" I said as I rolled my eyes. "Girl, you had on a white T-shirt, those Capri pants, and some slides. That wasn't good enough for your first time meeting somebody." "That's because maybe I don't want to meet anybody," I mumbled under my breath. "Let's go, Dani." She grabbed my hand and playfully pulled me out of her grandmother's front door. We both laughed as we headed down the street and around the corner. I got more nervous as we hit the street where we were supposed to meet the fellas. I mean, this was like a blind date. *What if I didn't like what I saw? What if my facial expression said at all?*

I didn't know what to think or what I was supposed to do. I was about to turn around just as I saw two guys appear at the other end of the street. They were headed right toward us. It was too late now. They were getting closer and closer to us. I noticed two things; one, I see why they called Black "black." Lol, and two, the cousin was handsome. The closer they got, the more I could see his physical attributes. He was taller than me with braids, light brown skin, bowlegged, and he had beautiful eyes. I was waiting to see one more thing. Yep, I needed to see him smile. He walked up, and my cousin said, "Hey Alley, this my cousin I was telling you about!" "What's up, how you doing? I'm Alley," he said. "Hi, I'm good. I'm Dani, Dani with an I," I replied. As soon as I said that, a grin spread across his face. It was a cute smile that exposed a small gap between the two fronts. "Nice to meet you Dani with an I." We both laughed. There was something strong and masculine about him, and his voice was deep. I started to wonder if he was my age... note to self - *ask that question!* We hit it off and the conversation was nice. I was so happy when he asked, "You look young, how old are you?" "I'm 15, and you look old, how old are you?" He laughed and replied, "D***, I look old?"

"I didn't mean it like that you just seem mature, so how old are you?" He kept chuckling and flashing his smile. "I'm 16." I got scared for a moment because I was afraid to talk to older guys. We talked a little bit more and then it was time for me to go. Alicia was eager to know how it went. "So, what do you think?" "I think he's cute. He seems cool," I said. She was satisfied with my answer and deemed herself as a great matchmaker. Lol. Summertime was fun and Alley and I talked on the phone and saw each other when we could. Alley was a dope boy and dope boys didn't go far from the corner because they didn't want to miss a sale. So, I'd go to my cousin's grandmother's house, and we'd go to see him at Black's. This was the basis of our relationship. I never saw him hustle, but 2+2 was adding up and equaling 4 again, so I knew what time it was. That lifestyle made it hard to go on dates or anything like that, and honestly hanging out in the hood was getting boring to me. I didn't smoke and I didn't like that he smoked either. He asked me to try it once, to which I said no, he asked again and I took the blunt, inhaled it, and blew it back out of my mouth like I was blowing out candles on a birthday cake. He chuckled and said, "Yeah you right, this ain't for you." Just then a dude rode by on a bike and yelled.

"Yo Al-lay!! What's up, boy??" Alley shouted something back in their hood language and they both laughed. He had a fun charming personality. Always smiling or laughing and everyone seemed to love him. I heard he was quick with his hands too, so I wouldn't let the personality fool you, lol! Although he was fun, and everything was going great, something was just missing and seemed like we could never connect. I believe that it was the fact that I was fresh off heartbreak and that his life was a little too fast-paced for me. Either way, I just couldn't focus on anyone else right then. I was about to start high school and I needed to get myself together, mentally and emotionally. My phone rang and I heard the voice on the other end say, "Dani with an I, lol, what you getting into today?" "I don't know Alley. In fact, tell me why they call you Alley?" I said. "It's short for Alec," he responded. "That's it? I guess I was expecting a hood story like you had to shake somebody down in an alley and they called you Alley ever since, lol."

"Man, girl you so funny, lol" We laughed for what seemed like forever, and slowly I felt the relationship guard I put up begin to come down. Hanging out with Alley was really cool and easy; yet, something was still missing, and I couldn't put my finger on it. Summer continued to stretch on, and I was still suffering on the inside. I wasn't sure if I was supposed to wait it out and the pain would disappear or if I was supposed to talk to someone. I figured I'd just wait and let my emotions sort themselves out. Meanwhile, I wondered how my dad was doing and how long it would be before I saw him again. He was on one of his disappearing acts. I think during these times I felt lonely the most. So much would happen in between the gaps where he was MIA. It only made me angrier and each time we reconnected it would be harder and harder to connect. I asked my mother to tell me the story of her and my father, which she happily agreed to tell. Here's how the story went. "Well,

I was 14 years old, and I had met up with my friend and her boyfriend. Your dad was there at my friend's house too. We liked each other, but we weren't dating at the time. I had a boy that I was seeing already, but I knew your dad really liked me. My friend was with her boyfriend and one thing led to another and me and Ron hooked up. We were just kids messing around and not really knowing much about anything… I ended up getting pregnant and I told my friend. Either she told him, or she told someone else and somehow it got back to him. He sat by me on the school bus one day and he asked if I was pregnant. I was nervous so I said, "What are you talking about?" So, he got this really angry look on his face, and he said that I had better stop telling people I was pregnant by him, or he was going to beat me up.

He was older and bigger than me and I was already nervous, but after that I was scared so I decided not to tell anyone else. I eventually had to tell my parents that I was pregnant, and Daddy held me down on the chair while Mommy slapped me across the face. They asked who the father was, and I was too afraid to tell them it was your father because everyone knew his family. His granddad was a great bishop in Jamestown, and his mom was also well-known. So, I told them your father was my boyfriend that I had at the time. He and his mother came by that Christmas after you were born when you were about eight months old. They brought you gifts and wanted you to be theirs, but my mother knew the moment she saw him that you weren't his. He and I broke up after that." There was such a sadness that came over her as she told that part, and I could tell she must've really cared for him. Maybe this is why she didn't like me because I was the cause of the breakup. I felt really bad but after a few moments of silence, she continued… "Years later, when you were a couple of years old, my mother's friend came over after picking up her son from the kindergarten school where your grandmother was a teacher. She had seen your dad's youngest sister at the school, and she said to my mother "Rocky, this child looks a lot like Nancy King's little daughter. I just saw the girl running around at the kindergarten. I froze when she said that. I heard my mother say, 'Child, Denise don't know who Dani's daddy is.' I wanted to say something, but I just froze."

After hearing that I felt even worse for my mom. I decided not to pressure her anymore because I didn't want to make her feel any worse. It made me feel even smaller knowing that my conception was a mistake. I mean these two people hooked up at a house party and never again. I got upset with my dad all over again. I decided to call him. It had been months already, I'm sure he wasn't still upset. I figured I needed to hear his side of the story. We ended up talking for hours, and when I asked him to tell me his version of how he and my mother got together, I was blown away. Not only did he confirm everything my mom had said, even the part about threatening to beat her up, but he went a step further to say this, "Yeah, you know I was young at the time, and I played the drums for my grandfather's ministry, and you know, it didn't look good for me to have a baby. You know to be the Bishop's grandson and in all honestly, I didn't want the responsibility. I didn't want to have to get a job. You know, I was young, and I never wanted children." I was speechless, tears swelled in my eyes, and I got a lump as big as a quarter at the back of my throat. I muted my phone so he couldn't hear me making sounds. He told the story with no regret, no remorse, and the only emotion I felt was frustration at the part where he expressed that he didn't want to have to get a job. His brutal honesty was like a knife to the heart, and I quickly regretted the fact that I even asked him. The fact that he never even went anywhere near the verge of saying, he wished he could do it all over again, and chose to father me and help my mother was scary. I realized that he was a selfish man who had no desire to apologize, nor take accountability for anything that he had done. Somehow in his mind, he had believed that he was some kind of victim in the situation.

He had no remorse for leaving a 14-year-old to deal with the repercussions of becoming pregnant, or the emotional, physical, mental, and financial responsibilities, and the psychological damage it caused my mother and me. This was the place where I lost respect for him as a man. I had never seen such an arrogant and pompous man! My siblings' fathers always seemed to take care of them. *My grandfather had never walked out on his family, so why was my dad like this? Who raised this guy?* I was so happy when the call ended. The next morning, I hugged my mom and told her how sorry I was that she had to go through that alone. I spent the rest of the day on the phone with Desiree talking about our plans for school. Here is when she dropped the ball on me. "Dani, there's this tech school I heard about and I'm going there instead of LBW. You gotta come with me. So now I'm confused because we were just about to start school shopping for clothes. "What do you mean tech school? What is so great about this school?" I asked. She proceeded to tell me we could go there and take classes that would lead to us getting jobs in the field in which we were taught. She said they had a cosmetology program where we could actually do clients' hair or there was an early childhood development class where we could interact with real kids in the school daycare. I had recently gotten into braiding hair and thought it would be cool to go into the cosmetology field like my Aunt Allie. The idea didn't sound so bad, I guess. "OK, so what about clothes? Are we still going to dress alike?" "Um that's the thing, they wear uniforms." Desi knew I was fed up with the uniforms, but I started to think… *my mom could barely afford to buy me enough uniforms. Why did I think I would be able to keep up with everyday changing of outfits if I went to LBW?*

My father still wasn't much financial help, and I was a fool for denying my mother of putting him on child support. I was a child, and being mindful of all the adults around me, not wanting him to think I only wanted to be in his life for money really messed me up. Anyway, the more I thought about it the more I became ok with the idea. The school was in my neighborhood, so I'd have to walk, but it was the same path as the one I took the previous year for middle school. "Ok Desi, let me ask my mother. I'll call you back." Of course, my mother thought it was a good idea too; so, I geared myself up to become a student at Gordon Academy of Technology! Blue dickies, red, white, and blue polo shirts, black or brown shoes, and ID badges… that was our uniform. Deep inside I didn't really want to go, but I was going to make the best of it for now. I was just going to focus on finishing and enjoying the rest of my summer. Nothing else major happened that summer, besides the fact that I was burying myself deeper inside myself until I was becoming unreachable, and I didn't even realize it. I was fully functioning to the naked eye, but I was putting up shields and walls of protection like no one could imagine. That's the summer I started to feel less like I fit in and more like a loner. Alley and I were cool, but it seems like the connection was more of a friendship. I mean we still considered each other boyfriend and girlfriend but couldn't find that place.

We would continue dating that summer and into the school year but then the unthinkable happened again. Alley ended up getting not one but two females pregnant. Here we go again, it's just like déjà vu! I was so upset… even though we had never gotten past go in the relationship, there was no sexual intercourse, no exchange of I love yous, no coming over to meet the family, none of that…but I still felt betrayed and hurt. I felt like I had lost a really close friend. I mourned the loss of that relationship for months. I trusted him and he played with me too. This was when I vowed to never ever date again. Why couldn't I just focus on school and my emotional stability? The answer to that question was "because I was still looking for love." I told myself to move on and forget about Alley and all that came with him. He ended up getting into some trouble and going to prison and I didn't see him again for over 20 years; and when I did, we'd walk past each other like we were strangers.

You ever wonder why cycles repeat itself in your life or in your family, why people begin the fight of their life in childhood, and they can't seem to break free? Its because the enemy came in and sowed a perpetual seed that's assignment is to keep you bound to that cycle, but there is deliverance through Christ!

CHAPTER 13

TRIED IT, DIDN'T LIKE IT

I strongly disliked my new school. I had had the notion that I would've been able to get into a cute cosmetology tech class, but because Desi and I decided to sign up late we had to take what was left. I ended up in AC and Refrigeration, and she ended up in Welding. Those classes were filled with boys. You would think that would make a girl happy but with all that I had experienced already… I was on the borderline of hating all men! I even side-eyed the bus driver because he was a man. This is how man-haters are born, long lines of women hurt by men. Up until this point, every man that I had a close relationship with had failed me, so I had no interest in taking this class. Luckily for me, we didn't have to take our tech class until sophomore year so maybe I could switch before then. Desi seemed to love it. Meanwhile, I just wanted to go home by the time the first bell rang. Lol. Things at home had started to become unbearable. My mother and I were like passing ships… one comes, one goes, and vice versa. We hardly ever had any meaningful conversations. She had a new boyfriend named Joseph, and this one seemed cool. He was older and didn't seem to be much of her type, but sometimes types change when you're tired of experiencing the same patterns as before. You end up not in a relationship for Love, but for other reasons. You settle just because you don't want to be alone, just to have companionship.

Joseph didn't have any money or swag, didn't have a car, or gold teeth and he seemed a bit older. So yes, this guy was different, but he was nice. He loved to cook, and he kept himself clean. He never said a harsh word to me. He just seemed like a man without ambition. He worked odds-and-ends jobs and at the local Family Dollar Store. He would bring my mom home small stuff from his job. At first, it was cute but after a while, I think she wanted more. Either way, I liked him. He didn't fight her, and I didn't hear of him cheating. He never sexualized me or abused us, and the dude could cook! There was something they were hiding but I couldn't figure it out. It's like they were sneaking around. Around that time my Aunt Deanna stopped coming around and I never heard my mother talking to her on the phone or leaving to go hang out with her anymore. What was going on? I think Mama dating Joe was the reason we almost never saw our aunt again.

I went to school one day and my cousin and I were talking about the dance team that we heard the school was putting together. There was no question whether or not we were going to try out for the team. Even though I was usually shy, dance and music were one way I could always express myself. Even as an adult one of my happiest times is when my kids and I turn on our Christian music and dance in our kitchen. G-Tech brought in an outside African Art Dancer named Londa. She would be our dance instructor. Everyone loved Londa. We went to tryouts and lined up in the back. We both made the team and before we knew it Londa had pulled both of us up to the front of the formation. We would be performing at all the basketball games, and I was so excited! I left tryouts in a happy mood and must not have been paying attention because when I cut the corner, I and this dude ran right into each other. He said excuse me and I snapped, "Dang, watch where you're going!" At this time, I still had a huge chip on my shoulder for men. He helped pick up my things that had dropped and said, "What's your name?" *Nope, not happening,* I thought to myself as I ignored his question. I just grabbed my stuff and walked away.

I met Desi in the hallway, and she had that look in her eyes. The one where she was about to rip somebody's head off. I walked up and asked her what happened. She had started going out with this dude from around my side. Apparently, something was going on with her and an ex-girlfriend of his. She and Desi were throwing some shade back and forth and of course, that meant we were instant enemies. Who are these chicks anyway? I was shocked to find out that they were a group of sophomores in my dance class! Great... I wasn't trying to make any enemies. I was at peace, wasn't bothering anyone, and no one was bothering me, but my friend was being bothered and that was definitely a problem! A problem with her was an automatic problem with me. That's how it went where we're from, loyalty is what it's called. Going back to dance practice wasn't an issue for me, but now I was just more alert. Honestly, no one was trying to fight with me or make smart comments or anything, but as time went on the beef between the two groups got bigger and bigger. Desi and the ex fought, and I and the ex's best friend had an altercation in the hallway. It was when classes were changing so the disturbance was big. One of us said something smart to the other and we charged toward each other, but so many students and teachers were around that nothing became of the fight.

Besides, she couldn't do anything with me anyway; I had the rage of a bull inside of me, and all I could see was RED. For the remainder of the year, we couldn't stand each other. As adults, I'd like to think that we still aren't childish enough to be holding on to that high school drama. All this was like déjà vu again, *but how did I get back here?* I had told myself that I wasn't going to do any of this again. No fighting, no dating, no drama! It seemed like no matter how I set out to do better, to be better, I just couldn't achieve success. *What was I doing wrong?* Around this time, I also felt anxiety and panic starting to flare back up in my life. Those voices that had told me to harm myself hadn't returned, but the panic definitely tried to revisit. I became very overly critical of myself again. I wasn't confident at all about anything except dance, and most of the time I wished I could shrink inside myself. I began to start panicking about whether my life was ever going to pan out. I didn't want to go through what my mother was going through. I told myself to breathe and go to class. I was just ready for the day to be over. My cousin Shay called that night talking to me about some dude she was talking to and how he had a friend interested in me. I said no! I got the whole speech again about not having to really like him and "just go with me please." I couldn't believe it was happening again like this. I can count 5 to 6 separate occasions where I was the date to a third wheel. Only this time it wasn't like Alley. I had absolutely no attraction to this guy at all. In fact, something about him really annoyed me and made my skin itch. I think I was allergic to him. Lol.

I played along for a short while, but I couldn't pretend for so long. I had to tell Shay that it wasn't for me, and she said she understood. I never really hung out with her and that boyfriend again. School was dragging along, but I was super excited for basketball season to start. We had been working hard on our routines and Londa felt that we were ready. Our uniform consisted of gray fatigue pants and airbrushed shirts with our names on them. My mom was able to give me the money for the uniform, but I needed a pair of white sneakers. She said no she didn't have the money. I rarely asked for anything but whenever I needed something it seemed like I couldn't get it. Shay told me not to worry because I could borrow her mid-top white Willie Deas. I agreed, but I didn't even think we wore the same shoe size anymore. I figured I could handle it. It would only be for a few minutes, right? Wrong! My feet burned the entire practice routine, but I pushed through it every week. My tolerance for pain was becoming way above the norm. Friday came and I was ready to get the week over. I had a science project that I had been working on and I was sure I was going to ace it. I was bummed out when I got my grade back and it was a C. I feel like I had worked hard on it, and it deserved a better grade, but at least it was a passing grade.

I went to lunch feeling upset about it. As I sat and waited for my friends, the guy who had bumped into me walked in. He nodded in my direction as he walked by. I nodded back and watched him walk across the cafeteria and dap up some of the fellas. I was cool with some of them, and some of them I didn't know. G-Tech was a technology school that bussed kids from the country, downtown, across town, and everywhere so it wasn't like my other schools where you knew just about everybody because y'all had grown up in the same hood. You were liable to meet somebody at the school that lived in Africa, lol. *Well, maybe not Africa, but you get what I'm saying.* I would continue to ignore him and not entertain any thoughts about having a boyfriend…until one day when a homeboy of his would approach me concerning him. "Yo Dani, what's up with you?" "Nothing much what's up with you?" "Chilling, look I'ma cut right to the point, my boy Q wants to talk to you. What do you think about him?" "What do you mean? I don't know him; I don't know anything about him. I don't think anything about him." I rolled my eyes. "See, here you go. Why you always gotta be so tough all the time? It was a simple question. Dang, girl, is he your type? Do you think he's cute? You wanna talk to him… any of these things?!" I laughed. "No, he's not my type, he's cute, and no I don't wanna talk to him. I don't want a boyfriend!" Paul was a clown so after I said all of that he busted out, "Ok, I will give him your number and tell him to call you!" Before I could say no, he got up and did the Deion Sanders across the cafeteria. I was beginning to think I had the word desperate written across my forehead because why did everyone feel the need to hook me up? I guess because everyone was hooking up and it seemed like that was all that was on everyone's minds. I saw people kissing in the stairway, guys hands on girls' butts, private areas being grabbed, hugging, and lots of sexual conversations during class. Everyone seemed over-sexual, so I guessed this was normal. We were in high school, and everyone's hormones were raging!

School ended for the day, and I set out on my walk home. We had a game, so I needed to get home, get dressed, and head back to school. That evening my mother's phone rang, and the voice on the other end said, "Hello, can I speak to Dani?" "This is me," I answered. We talked for like an hour and I remember thinking how by looking at him you would have thought he acted like a kid. He just looked very young. By conversation he seemed really chill, kind of shy, and laid-back. That was the beginning of the relationship, and it stretched to a year or so long. In the beginning, it was all good like most relationships. There were no red flags. He was sweet, caring, and kind and along the way, I gave myself to him like I had done in the relationship with Rich. I kept thinking to myself that this has to be forever because I don't want to be sexually active with any more people. The goal was to be married, to be a wife. For as long as I can remember, my goal was always to be a wife. I would turn out to be wrong about him too. He would play with my heart as well and we eventually broke up, but this time I had a broken heart during the relationship. The breakup would free me to meet the guy that I always wanted, the guy I needed. That guy would become my husband.

CHAPTER 14

ENOUGH, I WANT MORE

At first, Q was soft-spoken, kind of quiet, and shy like me. I didn't know what happened, but I could tell when the switch came. I started to hear little rumors about possible cheating. Conversations became less and his responses became short. It was almost like somebody was teaching him how to be a dog and I didn't like it at all! The school year had ended and because I had failed math with a 68, I could no longer attend G-Tech. You had to pass all your classes to stay enrolled at the school. I can't say that I was too upset, but I was worried about going to another school and leaving my boyfriend at a different school. Things were already shaky between us. I figured with me at another school he could be doing anything with anybody. Either way, there wasn't a choice, and I really don't know if I would have stayed if I could. Where I lived was zoned for LB Warriors, the original school that Desi and I were supposed to go to anyway. On top of having to go to another school, we were moving… Again. This time we were doubling back to the village, the place we lived, when I ran away and stayed next door. At this point, I didn't care. I was tired of trying to keep up with the emotions attached to the events of my life. From here on out I just needed to be a go-with-the-flow type of girl. So…we moved. I got a job at the neighborhood Winn-Dixie. I was so happy and super excited to have a job. I had turned 16 the previous April, so I was eligible to work. I love my job too, and I took it very seriously. If I was going to be a cashier, I was going to be the best. The vibe there was so lively and fun. People of all ages worked there. I would take my checks, cash them, iron my money, and put it in a shoebox.

I needed to have money to make sure I had clothes, shoes, and necessities for school. Everything was going well. We had moved and got settled in, and I would walk to work and walk back home, or sometimes my Granddaddy Charles would come to walk me home or pay for me to catch a cab. All of a sudden, my mother started snapping again. It's like she had two personalities. There were times when I wasn't doing anything, and she was just picking at me. I started to think she was on drugs or something for real now. I ended up moving back into my grandparents' house. I had been back and forth a few times when my mother and I needed time to cool off or space from each other, so it wasn't unusual. I packed up some stuff and headed back to Mason Street. It was easier to walk from their house to work anyway. My mother was so evil, she had a car and wouldn't take me to work; so, I was forced to walk or catch the city bus. I asked my grandparents what bill I could contribute to, to which they replied, "The phone bill because you use it more than us, lol." I'd pay them $60 toward the phone bill and I would save the rest of my money. I didn't see my mother or my sibs for most of that summer.

Things on Mason Street had changed. They were nicer to me now. I'm guessing that was because I was older. My Aunt Paris had given birth to two more sons, who my grandparents were taking care of, as well, and they were getting the abusive treatment now. I was in and out of the house with work and hanging out with Q, so I was kind of in my own world, but I felt sorry for the boys and Jack.

They didn't seem to have anyone that loved or cared for them except my grandparents, in their own weird way. That's where psychological manipulation came into play. It's like we knew they were wrong, but there was always that little voice that whispered "But if they hadn't taken you in what would have happened to you... You owe them!" That was the voice of Satan and the voice of the seeds our grandmother had planted. I always prayed my aunt would get free from her addiction and show up for the boys, but she never did. To this day, she is still addicted to drugs. I was determined to work hard and save my money and by the end of summer my determination paid off. I didn't have a whole lot of money, but I had enough to buy a couple of pairs of sneakers, a book bag, some sandals, and outfits for a couple of weeks. I hopped on the city bus by myself and went shopping at the mall and small outside stores like Fashion Cents. I felt good, responsible, and ready to start school. I only had one issue. My grandparents' house was zoned for another school; so somehow, we came up with a plan that I'd catch a cab, or my granddad would walk me to my mother's house, and I would catch the school bus from there in the mornings. I'd walk to work or walk over to my grandparents' house. The walk from my mom's house to my grandparents was approximately 25 minutes. The only thing I was afraid of was the dogs that could possibly chase me. While walking to my grandparents' house, a familiar truck pulled up and a familiar voice shouted. I turned around and I stared right in the face of Henry. It had been a while since I'd seen him. He had given me and my friends beer to drink one night many months ago when my mother wasn't home. My mother and my friend's mother were livid, so he was banned from coming over. I wasn't sure why he had been there in the first place.

"No thanks, Henry I'm good!" "Girl, get in this car, how do you think your Mama would feel if she knew I was out here and saw you walking and didn't give you a ride? I was hesitant, but I figured he was right. I got into his car, and we headed to my grandmother's house. On the way, he tried to make small conversation, but I was determined to stick to the objective of just getting a ride home, so I kept quiet. He remarked on my mole being a beauty mark and I still ignored him. We pulled up to my grandparents' house and I jumped out quickly. To my surprise, he pulled up the next day, as well. Again, I accepted the ride. This time his conversation was more aggressive, and I vowed never to step foot in his vehicle again. "Hey Dani, do you know you're beautiful? You look like a model. You look better than your D*** mama girl! You're so beautiful. If I hadn't of met your mama first, we could have…" I yelled "Could have nothing!! How dare you!!" We pulled up to my grandparents' house and this time I jumped out. I told him not to ever offer to pick me up again and slammed his door. That was the last time I saw him on my walk home. I appreciated my Granddad though because

I knew it was a sacrifice to scrape together cab fare for a whole week, every week, to get me to school every morning. I told myself that I would repay them when I could.

Another summer ended and another school year started. Life had sped up at this point and I just wanted to make sure I was keeping up. I went to school and loved it. It was so familiar to me, nothing like the bougie G-Tech. I had three male cousins who went to LBW too. David Jr, his big brother, Andre, and our other cousin, Maurice. David Jr and I weren't really close at the time, but my other cousin and I were. Both Andre and Mari looked out for me. Andre and I were our grandmother Evangelist King's oldest two grandchildren. We were born five days apart, me on the 17th and him on the 22nd. He introduced me to a lot of people at the school, because I only knew the people from around my way. Everyone seemed cool. I liked my language arts class the most. It was full of people to laugh and joke with. I still promised myself that I'd stay focused because I now had to catch up. Since I failed my math class the previous year, I had a ninth-grade math, and all the rest were sophomore classes. My homeroom was a ninth-grade homeroom as well since I had a ninth-grade core class. Technically this was supposed to be my Junior year!! Sigh I needed to catch up and do it quickly. I cut out all the class clowning and focused on my work. There was this boy in my language arts class named Jermaine. I thought he was so handsome! I mean he was FINE! He was tall and bowlegged with braids. He had this beautiful skin and white teeth that matched a gorgeous smile. The color of his skin was reddish brown. I can't explain it, but I likened it to a reddish-brown brick color. He was clean and well dressed, and he smelled like he walked straight out of a cologne bottle… in a good way. I never smelt guys my age who smelled like cologne. Laundry detergent and fabric softener, yes, but sweet like this? Absolutely not! It sparked my interest as to who this guy was and where he came from. Who was raising him because he seemed so masculine and mature? I couldn't entertain any of that though because technically I was still talking to Q, even though he was blowing me off every chance he got.

Jermaine was easy to trip with and easy to talk to, so we became friends quickly. We were not inappropriate and never took it outside of school. He knew I had a boyfriend, and he didn't know I had even checked him out on that level. I did think he was a little arrogant though, but the closer we got the more I realized it was more of confidence than arrogance. He knew what he wanted, what kind of girl he wanted, and he knew what he didn't want. He was not the type to settle for less and he was ambitious and goal-oriented. He didn't do or sell drugs, but he had a real job and his own money. Again, who was raising this young grown man? Lol? We'd meet up and walk either to class or to the cafeteria. I never heard any of the girls say they had messed with him or dated him. I wondered why he didn't have a girlfriend. I didn't ask, I just figured it would eventually come up in conversation. I found myself anticipating the times when we'd see each other. The relationship was so pure, and for a small minute, I began to wonder if he liked me too. I was killing it at this point! School, work, social life, and for the first time in a while, I felt happy. I just couldn't figure out this thing with Q. One day I called his house phone and he answered "YEA?" That wasn't how he usually answered the phone, so I asked him some necessary questions. "Hey, what's up with you? You don't answer your phone like that. Honestly, I feel like you've been blowing me off a lot lately." There was a pause and then an agitated response.

"What? What are you talking about? Nobody blowing you off and I don't even wanna argue with you about this, matter of fact, I'll call you back!" Click! I became overwhelmed with anger, so I dialed his number back Ring… Ring… Ring… No answer. I called back again prepared to cuss him out Ring… Ring… Ringggg… No answer. I was furious, so angry that I started to cry. I always cried when I got angry, and then directly after, I'd snap. Instead of snapping, I just dried my face and decided I was fed up with his childish ways. I thought strongly about breaking up with him the next time I spoke to him. A couple of hours went by and then the phone rang, and his number flashed across my caller ID. This is it. I was ready to let it loose. I answered the phone and the voice said, "I'm sorry. Look, it's not you. I've got some other things going on, I apologize. Can you forgive me?" This made it difficult for me to say anything that I had wanted to say. All I could say was "I forgive you."

That was the beginning of toxic behavior that so many of us accept. They offend, and then they apologize. You forgive them and then they do it all over again. The cycle of abuse continues… and it did continue to happen, repeatedly. I started to think he was cheating also because the conversations became fewer, as well. If I had continued to accept the behavior, he still would've been stringing me along. It seems like he thought he could do whatever he wanted, and I would still be around. He'd soon find out that was untrue. The next day in Language Arts class, I and my group of classmates got into a discussion about dating and relationships. No one knew what I was experiencing in my relationship because I hid it and spoke highly of it to them. The classmate said he didn't think it was possible to have a faithful relationship with two people attending two different schools. He turned to me and said, "Come on now, do you really think your boyfriend is being 100% faithful to you at a different school?" That comment made me furious because I knew what I was going through in the relationship and at that moment I thought everyone else did too. In my mind that comment made everyone stop and stare at me. What I was already thinking had now become a reality to me when he made that comment. I was embarrassed, especially because Jermaine was there. I didn't talk to anyone for the rest of the day.

Meanwhile, math was kicking my butt and I decided I needed to focus on that. I don't know why I didn't get a tutor. The thought just didn't cross my mind. Interim reports ended up coming out and I had a 65 in math. With my track record in math, I guess my grandmother thought it was appropriate to contact my mother and let her know. Of course, she fussed, and I explained that it was only interims and that I would bring the grade up before report cards. She insisted that work and school couldn't co-exist and that I needed to quit my job and focus on my math. It seemed like she just wanted to take away everything that made me happy. My mother was becoming evil and vindictive toward me. She had begun to move erratically. Something was just off. She made me quit my job because I was 16 and still a minor. I thought to myself, *I don't even live with her anymore so how does she get to run my life?* I begged my grandmother not to make me quit, but she said she didn't want to go over my mother's decision.

I think if she had known my mom would have acted that way, she probably would've waited it out to see what my report card looked like. Life was so unfair; nothing ever went in my favor. I had even tried going to church looking for answers. I became a member of my family's church. Bishop King had passed away, and my grandmother, the evangelist, was now the pastor. I would go to church Sunday after Sunday and go up to the altar crying. I didn't have a relationship with God yet, so I was hoping that someone would hear from God on my behalf with instruction; but God never spoke to me, so every Sunday I left the same way I came… broken. After I had to quit my job, I did what I always did, sucked it up and kept it moving. I'd always taken care of my things so I could get by for a while with the clothes that I had. I even ironed and folded my underwear, lol. I was determined not to let anything break me. School was going by in a blur and Christmas break was approaching. I was happy to have that break. I think all the students were. On the last day of school Jermaine and I said our goodbyes. I wasn't looking forward to not seeing or talking to him for weeks, he dapped me up and told me he'd see me when we got back to school.

All I could think about was what he'd be doing during his break time. There was something so different about the way I was feeling about him. I never felt this feeling about anyone else before, but I had to suppress those feelings because I was still in a relationship... if that's what you wanted to call it. I started thinking about ways to officially end it. The obvious fact was that it was already over, I just didn't want to believe it or have the courage to end it. One day after Christmas, it all came full circle. For Christmas, he had bought me a gift, which was kind of shocking since we were barely communicating so I thought, *ok, maybe things are going to work out after all.* One particular day I called and got blown off again. We got into an argument and that's when I told him I didn't think it was going to work out anymore. I realized whatever I allowed was what was going to continue to happen! I got tired of the behavior. "What, so it's like that?" "Yes! yes, it's like that! You act like we even talk now, and I would hear things about you messing around with other girls!" We continued to argue for a little bit and hung up. I'm sure he probably thought I needed time to cool off, but I was serious. Watching my mother go through one toxic relationship after the next was enough for me to know I didn't want to repeat those patterns when choosing who I wanted to be in a relationship with.

At first, I felt bad for just dropping it on him like that but then I thought about how he didn't care about my feelings, and all of a sudden there was a weight lifted off my shoulders. *Dear Reader, never stay where you're not wanted.*

I enjoyed the rest of my break and couldn't wait to get back to school. On the first day back, the bell rang for language arts class, and I couldn't wait to get there. I had gotten a pair of pink and white Air Max for Christmas, so I wore them with a gray sweatpants outfit with a pink T-shirt underneath. I got my hair relaxed so my hair was sitting cute and healthy, about shoulder length, down my back. I walked in and said what's up to everybody and looked to the back seat where he sat. There he was with a fresh pair of Jordans and a dark gray hooded sweatpants outfit! I guess great minds think alike. We said what's up to each other, and I sat in my seat, which was directly in front of his. I turned around and shot him a smile.

He later would tell me he was trying to figure out why I was doing that because that was unusual for me. LOL! I told him I had broken off the relationship and we talked about that for a minute. I must've been smiling way too much because our teacher Ms. Blake said in front of the class "Well Jermaine, it looks like you have an admirer. Someone keeps smiling at you. Dani, move to the front of the class please." I could have screamed, lol. Instead, I owned it and smiled at him one more time before I moved to the front. Our friendship continued to blossom and my cousin Andre, Jermaine, and I would talk three-way on the phone every day. I wasn't sure if Jermaine would make a move or if he even liked me, for that matter. I told my cousin that I started to like him, but I wasn't going to be aggressive and holler at him, so I came up with a plan, lol. The next time we would all get on the phone, he would ask us if we liked each other and if we wanted to go out. With fingers crossed I joined the call that day. All I knew was if he said no, I was going to throw my phone away, lol. We both ended up saying yes and from that moment, January 11, 2002, we became inseparable.

CHAPTER 15

A LOVE LIKE THIS

To this day, choosing to date, love and marry Jermaine was the best decision I'd ever made, besides my decision to give my life to the Lord. Outside of the love of God, It has been Jermaine's love that has saved me. He was the one God had kept for me. The way he has loved and cared for me from the beginning to the present day has been nothing short of intentional and amazing. I can say with all honesty he's been the only male who hasn't broken me and my heart. Young ladies, pray and ask God to send you your mate. Don't rush into or settle in a relationship that God did not design for you. Trust the Lord and allow him to send the Man He has for you. Also, pray and ask God to make you a wife of good character, of love and resource, a wife that mirrors the Proverbs 31 Woman. Ask God for complete healing and wholeness so you will be the best that you can be.

Jermaine and I became inseparable. We liked each other and enjoyed spending time together. We always had each other's backs. It was a sweet kind of Love. He was very loving and attentive. When he found out that I was skipping lunch at school because they didn't have what I liked to eat, he'd buy me chicken sandwiches, French fries, Otis Spunk Cookies, and Fruitopia drinks. When he found out I walked from one destination to the next after I got off the school bus, he started giving me cab fare every day, so I didn't have to walk. I never asked nor did I have to ask for anything. For Valentine's Day, he sent 100 red heart balloons, four boxes of candy, a teddy bear, and two cards to me at school. He had multiple people deliver them to me in class like a delivery service. I had so much stuff that the school made me leave it all in the front office until dismissal. No one had ever made me feel that special in my life. My mother was upset when she saw all of the things for Valentine's Day and asked me a silly question. "He's doing all this for you. What are you doing for him?" I ignored her. We went on our first date in March, and this was the day I knew that I was in love with him. We went ice skating and to dinner. The restaurant was within walking distance, so we decided to walk there. As we did, he very appropriately walked behind me with his arms draped around my neck.

We laughed and talked the entire time. He reached around and kissed my cheek and neck. I felt a safety in his arms that I'd never felt before. It turned out this would be both of our official first dates and to me it was perfect. I got caught up so quickly in his love that I realized everything before him was truly puppy love. I seemed to forget about all the betrayal and heartache I had experienced before. The love was so real that it was unreal. It also brought out a lot of haters and girls coming out of the woods at him. All of a sudden, since he and I started dating, every week a different girl was telling him how they "always liked him." For the most part, I thought it was funny but there was this one persistent girl. She slid her personality picture on his desk with a message on the back. After class, he gave it to me and told me what she did. I had put the old fighting me to rest, but I could feel her trying to rise up again. Some females could be so daring. I could never respect a female who deliberately went after another female's guy. I wasn't worried about Jermaine because he never gave me a reason to question his faithfulness. But females, oh they were the ones that I didn't trust. Some other things transpired throughout the remainder of the year. She would also try to get him to date her cousin. This chick was super bold. Tensions continued to rise…

Valentine's Day came, our first date, us meeting each other's family and spending every moment together. Throughout all this, he continued to charm and love his way into my heart. I believed he was feeling the same way about me. My birthday came around and he SPOILED me. He bought me three pairs of sneakers, one matched a pair of his, three outfits to match the sneakers, a huge XO bracelet, which was very popular at the time, five rings, balloons, flowers, and cards! That weekend I lied to my grandparents and told them I was spending the night at Shay's. He surprised me with dinner and a hotel. He had all the gifts laid out in the room. Even though we had fallen in love, and were maturing into young adults, we often say that we shouldn't have done those things the way we did them. I wasn't aware of the spiritual consequences of fornication and lying at the time. The Bible says in Revelations 21:8 KJV "but the fearful, who doubt God and the unbelieving, the abominable and the murderer, whoremongers, sorcerers, idols, and all liars shall have their part of the lake which burns with fire and brimstone, which is the second death."

It also says that fornication is sex before marriage and is a work of the flesh that denies you access into the kingdom of God. I wouldn't receive this knowledge until later but as for you, I tell you now, flee youthful lusts, and save yourself for marriage. If you've already given in to sexual immorality, purify yourself by becoming abstinent, and stay away from all further sexual immorality. God loves you. The following day was a Sunday and I hung out at his mom's house with him like we usually did on the weekend. We did more in the first six months than most adults. I took him to meet my mother for the first time, and the visit was very unpleasant. We were dressed alike in black and white Jordans with matching outfits, and I had on all the jewelry he had gotten me for my birthday. We were looking good and feeling even better. We pulled up to my mother's spot. I should have known that this was going to be a bad idea. My mother despised me, so why did I think she would embrace him?

We got out of the car and knocked on the door. She opened the door, looked him up and down, and said through the screen door, "And who are you?" He greeted her and pulled his hand out to shake hers. She kept the door shut. I said, "Mama this is my boyfriend." Before I could say anything else she said, "You don't have no boyfriend!" and slammed the door. I felt overwhelmed with embarrassment and confused again. I could feel tears well up in my eyes, and that pesky lump in my throat. I didn't understand why she was so mean to me. It was at that moment I realized that she was never going to accept me, so I would need to ween myself off the need to be accepted and loved by her. I was tired of the Jekyll and Hyde routine. I convinced myself I was on my own now and I believe that at that moment I became a little colder. That's another reason why Jermaine was my superhero.

My mother and my birthdays were three days apart, so she celebrated hers on April 20. She chose to go out the following weekend. She asked me to come over and stay with my brothers and sisters while she went out. I was supposed to be hanging out with Jermaine so she told me he could come over to her house. Jekyll and Hyde again! Monday, we got the door slammed in our face and Friday he could come over. This lady was so confusing; nevertheless, we took her up on the offer. Lol. This wouldn't be the end of her Jekyll and Hyde act though. One day I got off the school bus and I decided to go to her house for a visit instead of going straight home to my grandparents. Sometimes I would stop by there to talk to Jermaine on the phone before he went to work. That day I walked into the house dressed in the red & white Jordans with the matching red & white outfit, all the jewelry on my fingers and neck, my hair was done, and I was looking cute and feeling really confident. I picked up the phone and dialed Jermaine's number and we began to converse. Like a crazy person, my mother came rushing out of her room. She started asking me crazy questions like "What did I give up for the stuff that he was buying for me?" I felt really offended and I asked her what she was talking about. She kept trying to reach for my hand to take the phone. "Let me speak to Jermaine" is all she kept saying.

When I kept saying no, she got angrier and angrier. She backed me up into the wall, put her finger against my head to mug me, and said, "Don't play with me, little girl." Standing face to face, looking into her eyes, and listening to the sound of her voice, I saw an evilness that was increasing in intensity towards me, and I realized she was trying to provoke me so she could fight me! It changed from a mother-and-daughter situation to a woman-to-woman situation where I needed to defend myself. I could hear Jermaine on the other end of the phone saying, "Just don't say anything, don't say anything to your mother!" I started to feel really threatened and I told Jermaine I'd call him later. I put down her phone, picked up my book bag, and walked out of the door. That was it. It was the last straw for me. I decided that I would never go back there again. I didn't see my mother again for a few months and the only reason I did was because I got pregnant and had a miscarriage. The ambulance drove me from my grandmother's house to the hospital and I could see out the ambulance's back door. I saw my mother's blue van behind us. Jermaine was the shift leader at his place of employment. He was able to leave and come to the hospital and stay as long as he could. He left and went back to work so he could finish his shift. Of course, my mother made a big deal of it. It seems like any time she could find something, she tried to use it against us. I argued with her that I understood why he had come and had to leave, and I felt that she was making a big deal out of something that wasn't that big of a deal. I had lost my first baby and the feelings of that left me feeling depressed and sad and here she was wanting to argue with me at a time like this. I just wanted the whole situation to be over so I could move on. School ended and summer came. I was so proud of myself for passing my classes!

Now that summer was here, I could go back to work, which was another plus. Jermaine and I talked about our plans for the summer. It would be our first summer together. Along was so many other qualities and attributes that attracted me to him was the fact that he was so masculine, and he played instruments like the keyboards and drums. He didn't look like a musician to me. He had too much swag, lol. One day before we started dating, I found out he was a musician when he entered my chorus class, sat on the piano bench, and began to play "All My Life" by KC and JoJo. Andre and I started singing and harmonizing. He continued to play songs by Carl Thomas, Jagged Edge, and Usher. We sang along to all of them, he began to play "The Storm Is Over Now" by Kirk Franklin. There was a male and female duet with the choir singing the chorus. Andre and I killed the duet. Jermaine later told me that when he heard me singing that song, he heard the sound and knew that was a sign to make me his girl. The masculine characteristics came into play when he stood up to protect me and he also knew how to tame me, lol. I was still a tiny bit sassy and operating out of whatever toxic behavior I had been raised around. Nothing too major, I just needed to learn how to tame my tongue. My grandmother used to say cuss words like they were part of the dictionary! Her mouth was reckless and should've been a registered weapon.

I've heard multiple New York natives say that's just how New Yorkers speak...harsh and curse words, lol. So, I chalked it up to that, but I also picked it up. It would mostly come out of me when I was angry. I never really noticed that he didn't curse until one day we were on the phone and got into a small disagreement and I began to curse at him. He asked me to stop, but I was so angry I kept going. He said, "If you keep cussing at me, I'm going to hang up on you!" and that's exactly what he did. I would call back three times fussing and cussing and he would hang up each time. Even though I was right about the argument, he felt disrespected and made sure I knew it. The last time I called back I stopped cussing, and we worked out the situation. I've been delivered from cursing ever since! It took him to tell me that I was behaving in a toxic manner, and he was not accepting it from me.

Ladies, trust a man who puts you in your place respectfully and calls you out of your toxic generational patterns and behaviors. If he is not telling you anything wrong and is helping you heal emotionally, listen to what it is he is saying.

I remember the last time I went to visit Jermaine at his mother's house before the move. He had been in contact with a friend who needed a roommate and was considering moving out. Things weren't so great at his house, and when he and his mother got into a disagreement over the air conditioning, I think that was the last straw. The next day he moved out of his mother's house and into an apartment with his new roommate. It was not long after that when I started spending the night with him. My grandparents had agreed to it, but my mother did not know about it. That was very unusual for them to allow me to spend the night with him at his place and I wondered what would make them say yes to something like that. It turns out my grandfather had gone up to Jermaine's job multiple times asking to borrow money to pay bills. Their bills and my mother's bills. At first, I wasn't aware, but when Jermaine told me, I was so upset. His exact words were "It's like they're pimping you out. As long as I give them money, you can come over freely." I'm just glad he was a good dude because what if he wasn't? I could have been getting abused and they would have pushed me to stay with him because of the money. This did nothing for my self-esteem!!

Then they switched it up and said I was spending too much time with him. Their method of stopping me from going over would cause me to largely distrust my grandfather. Our relationship never returned to the way it was after this incident. He went to Jermaine's job and proceeded to try and convince him to tell me I shouldn't come over so much. When Jermaine refused, my grandfather said in a muffled voice, "You know if you wanted to get a girl on the side, I wouldn't say anything." Jermaine replied, "No sir, I wouldn't do anything like that." My family continued to devalue and degrade me, and I had had enough. I confronted my grandparents, and my grandfather didn't deny anything. Instead, my grandmother jumped to his defense. "So, I guess Jermaine runs and tells you everything like a little B****!!!" That was it, I had to get away from these people! Jermaine and I didn't let what anybody was trying to do break us. We worked, spent time together, and grew increasingly in love every day. I began to crave him so badly when we weren't with each other. It was more than sexual, just to be in his company was all I needed. Eventually, I did the unthinkable. At 17 years old, I decided to move out of my family's house and move in with my boyfriend. I did not know God's standards, or that what I was doing was wrong. Jermaine knew, but he just wasn't living a life of obedience to God's Word at the time. Because I wasn't aware, I put my soul at risk of being lost. The Bible says that my people are destroyed for the lack of knowledge. Moving out was satisfying to my flesh and even though he was the one and it felt so good, in the eyes of God, it was so wrong.

Trouble was brewing, and my mother was the one stirring the pot. I got a call from my grandparents stating that my mother said I had to come back home. Somewhere during a conversation with Jermaine's roommate, my grandfather mentioned that if he didn't bring me back, they would get the law involved. Something about statutory rape was mentioned as well. When he found out, he was very torn about what to do. He didn't want to take me back but now threats of law enforcement and charges against him called for concern. He was 17 years old and so was I, but we didn't know the laws. It sounded funny to me, though, because I remember that my mother had moved out at 16 years old with my brother's father, who was twice her age. My father also visited Jermaine's job that day with a plea to take me back, but he came from a spiritual standpoint. After talking to my dad, he decided it would be best to take me back. I understood why he was doing it, but it didn't stop me from feeling like they had cornered him, and I felt betrayed.

Jermaine promised that it was not going to change anything and that we'd still spend the same amount of time together, and then, when we turned 18 years old, we'd get our own place together. Then he said, "Your grandmother said that everything would be the same, and nothing would change." With a serious face, I looked at him and said, "You don't know them." He looked back at me with a nervous look like he was asking "What does that mean?" I had all my things packed and we got into his roommate's car and drove in the direction of my grandparents' house. Neither of us said a word the entire ride. Tears began to fall from my eyes not because he had agreed to take me back, because I understood the reason, but I had suffered so severely from abandonment and rejection, that any and every sign of it sent me deep into the sad place inside of me. It felt like rejection and abandonment. It was another car ride back to the PLACE OF BROKENNESS. We got back to my grandparents' house, and I thought, *Here I am back on Mason Street.*" Jermaine and I said our goodbyes and when I got into the house, I exploded. All of the feelings I had been feeling came rushing out. I kicked and screamed and beat on the walls and the furniture. I screamed and cried. It was so uncontrollable that I couldn't even stop myself and my grandfather came in yelling, "Girl shut up before I whoop you with this extension cord!" I cried even more and yelled, "I'm not staying here.!"

"Shut up girl.!" He yelled. This went on for about 20 minutes until I exhausted myself. They came to my room and pulled the phone out of the wall and yelled that I was not going to be able to see or talk to him again and that I couldn't leave the house or use the phone. I remember thinking to myself the next day that I was going to get up, jump the locked gate, and walk away from this place for the final time. There was no way I was going to become a prisoner again. I just wanted to be free.

I got up the next day and waited for a chance to use the phone. While my grandfather was out that evening, and my grandmother was in her room, I snuck to the phone. As I picked it up and started dialing, I could hear Jermaine's voice on the other end saying, "Hello. Hello." We had been calling each other at the same time. I told him how they lied to him about nothing changing and how they said I could not see him, use the phone, or leave the house. He told me how he waited at the gas station across from my house the night before to see if I would come out and if I had, he would've taken me back and faced whatever came after that. He had been calling all night and all day and couldn't get an answer. I told him that they had taken the phone out of my room and restricted me from touching it.

The next thing he would say would make me fall even deeper in love with him as I realized the effort and tenacity that he put into being able to bring me back to him. There was a police officer who lived in the neighborhood where he and I had moved in with his roommate. He told me how he sat on the curb for hours, waiting for the officer to come out to ask him about the minor laws as they pertained to us moving out and living together. When the officer came out, he was surprised to see that it was our school resource officer, Officer D. She had grown very fond of us during school, and the feeling was mutual. It turns out that the officer who lived in the neighborhood was Officer D's boyfriend, and she had been over for a visit. He told her everything that had transpired. She told him that, by law, once we turned 17 years old, we were considered adults, and that I had passed the age of consent, which was 16 in South Carolina.

At age 17 our parents couldn't legally kick us out, but we could legally leave home. She assured him that no charges could be brought against him or me for anything. He was relieved and couldn't wait to talk to me to let me know. The last thing he said to me before we hung up was "Let your people know I'm coming to get you. I love you." This man's love for me would stay deep and consistent to the day of writing this book 22 years later. The love of a good man can heal you in places you didn't know you hurt! My husband held a portion of my healing and deliverance within himself and God held my wholeness...

CHAPTER 16

MIXED EMOTIONS

I told my grandmother that I was leaving and gave her all the information that Jermaine had learned from Officer D. She was upset, but not really. What I got from her was almost like a "let her go" type of vibe. It appeared that my mom was pushing this as she had called my dad and grandfather to do all her dirty work. Now it was time to face the one behind all the drama. My grandmother decided that if I was going to leave, I would leave my mom's house and not hers. "That's between you and Denise," she said. We took a cab to my mother's, and the evening would stretch into the early morning hours of the next day. Jermaine had been waiting for my call. He became concerned when he didn't hear from me. The meeting at my mother's house would consist of a lot of yelling, screaming, and crying. She would never really give me a true reason as to why she wanted me to stay at home. Just a whole lot of "you're not grown." I added it up to be about control and her own unhappiness. She never seemed like she wanted me around before anyway and I believe she didn't want me to be happy because she was miserable. *Who was I to have found love and stability when she was still looking for it?* She never spoke to me from a motherly standpoint. It was never 'I care for you, and I don't want you to make a mistake by moving too fast. It was always from the standpoint of a jealous enemy. I'd catch her looking at me from across the room with a sour face that read, "I can't stand her."

She had done this since I came to live with her, and it would continue. I felt that if I had fallen in love with someone who would've done me wrong, she would have been thrilled. We argued into the early hours of the morning and exhausted each other. She would go the last mile to prove I was unlovable and that nobody wanted me. Between the hours of 3-4 am she rang Jermaine's phone, who had fallen asleep after waiting for me to call. When he answered, it wasn't my voice he heard. My mother had given up after not being able to change my mind, but she had one more card to play. She figured she'd call him and talk him out of accepting me back. "Jermaine I'm just calling because I wanted to know if you really want Dani to come back." I couldn't hear his responses, but I knew he was telling her yes by the look on her face. She didn't stop there, she acted as if I wasn't even there. "Jermaine you're a good-looking young man. You have a good head on your shoulders and a lot going for yourself, you can do better than Dani. Don't let Dani ruin your life. Do you really want her to come back?" At that moment she made me feel the lowest that I've ever felt. There was no lower to go. As I held back tears, I blacked out and didn't hear another word she said. I just knew that when daylight came, I was going to walk out of her house and never come back.

Jermaine stuck to his responses of wanting me back and it infuriated her. She slammed the phone down in his ear and looked at me so coldly and said, "Get Out, you wanna leave? There's the door!" I walked out of the door into the darkness in my bedclothes with no phone, no money, no nothing. She didn't even wait until the sun came out or allow me to use the phone to call Jermaine. At this point, I was so physically, emotionally, and mentally drained. I walked up and down her street waiting to see if someone would come outside so I could ask to use their phone. The sun came up after I had been outside for about two hours. It was summertime so nobody was getting up early to go to school and it was too early to knock on anyone's door, so I waited. Just when I figured I'd start walking, one of my brother's friends walked up the street. I went over and asked him if I could use his cell phone. I immediately called Jermaine and he was shocked to know that I had been outside for hours, he told me to call a cab and he would pay when I got there. When the cab came, I got in and looked out the window back at the house. I thought about my siblings. I thought that maybe my mom would have been looking out the window with remorse for what she had just done, but the door was shut, and the blinds were tightly intact. I rode away in tears. I cried for the little girl inside of me who would never know what it was like to be loved by her parents. I cried because I felt like a piece of trash that had been left by the roadside. I cried because the woman who carried me in her womb, had never carried me in her heart. I cried because I was tired.

When the cab pulled up to Dorchester Oceans Apartments I got out as he paid the cabby. As it pulled off, I collapsed into his arms. He told me my eyes were so red and puffy, and that he had never seen me like that before, but the relief that came over my body as he held me was undeniable. That was it. I moved out for good and, for a while, completely detached from my family. I never returned. I worked and paid my portion of the bills. Jermaine, his roommate, his roommate's girlfriend, and I got along really well. They were cool people from Fitzgerald Georgia. Will worked with Jermaine at the local Sonic Drive-In and Will's girlfriend Nisha came down on the weekends. We kicked it and everything was cool. One night after work. I went to Jermaine's job to wait for him to get off like I did every night. We didn't have a vehicle yet so Will would take us home. It was convenient because my job was close to where they worked. That particular night, the girl with whom the tensions had been rising, pulled up to pick up her check. I looked at her and she looked at me. I mouthed to her, "What are you looking at?" She smiled at me with a silly look on her face. That was enough to send me. I got up and punched her off the patio. The fight began and we ended up in the parking lot. Nisha was there and broke us up….eventually. I didn't feel bad after this fight like I usually did because I felt 100% provoked, but I did start to wonder if there would come a time when I would learn to let things roll off my back.

I would like to welcome that peaceful energy into my life. Young ladies with so many stresses in life. It can really bring you down, but thankfully, we can turn to the word of God for light and scriptures that can encourage, uplift, teach, and inspire us as women to be the women

God called us to be. 1 Peter 3: 4 says, "Let us know that our beauty does not only come from the adornment of our outside, but also a gentle, calm, quiet spirit, which is of great worth to God. I wanted very badly to get back to that place. I know that I wasn't always controlled by my trauma and anger. A quote about me from my absolute favorite teacher reads ….

"If you didn't know, you were the apple of my eye!!! You were one of the reasons that made me want to teach. I knew that you were going to be the child who would have a bright future. You always gave/did your best. You showed at a young age that you could listen for understanding and perform the task(s) at hand. I loved the way that you WANTED to learn new things. You had such a calm and loving spirit. Forever my STAR STUDENT" -Alethia Jefferson

Anger is a tough emotion to face. Without the proper tools to cope with it, one may turn to the same toxic patterns that they experienced growing up, to deal with it, or they completely hold it in and neither one of these is the healthier choice. I wish I had known that I could turn to the scriptures to calm the anger and extinguish the rage. Ladies and gentlemen, the Bible (Ephesians 4:26-27) says that it's OK to be angry, but you must not let that anger produce sin. Psalm 37:8 says Don't give in to worry or anger; it only leads to trouble. James 1: 19-20) says Everyone should be quick to listen, slow to speak, and slow to become angry because human anger does not produce the righteousness that God desires. Proverbs 14:17 says people with hot tempers do foolish things, but wise people remain calm. I tell you this because I didn't know, and I feel that knowing the Bible was alive and holds the scripture for any and everything you face would has been beneficial to me in my trying times. I would have known that I was not alone, and that God was with me every step of the way. and even navigating my path. I look back now and can identify that He was there all the time.

Jermaine and I continued to work the entire summer in preparation for starting the next school year. Because we moved out, we were not zoned for our school anymore, so a friend of the family who worked nearby volunteered to pick us up and take us to school every day. We just had to find a ride home. That worked for about a week. We hadn't made any preparations because we thought the friend of the family was a solid means of transportation, but he wasn't, and we ended up having to leave school. It wasn't necessarily a choice we wanted to make, especially because I had worked hard to catch up. At the time I was still estranged from my family, and we didn't think that we could have transferred to the zoned school or catch the city bus to a nearby neighborhood that was zoned for the school and just rode their school bus. We did make plans to go back once we had a vehicle, which would end up being a few months later, but the truth is by that time we had settled into the adult life of working and paying bills. Years later in our adulthood, we both tried to go back to Fishburne Education Center to receive our high school diplomas, but scheduling and lack of childcare would cause us to stop schooling again. So that's where we were… working, living, and loving, and in February 2003 all of our loving became evident when we got pregnant for the second time and prepared to welcome a baby in the upcoming fall of that year.

I was so excited. I thought that I finally had someone that was mine. Someone besides Jermaine, of course, that I would love and take care of and would love me. Someone that no one could take away from me. I made a vow that I would be nothing like my mother nor cause the trauma she caused me. I will not pass that down to my children. The toxic behavior stopped with my parents! We began to get our life ready to welcome a baby. A little before we found out, Jermaine's roommate had decided to move back to his hometown, so we had a small window of time to get our own place. Everything was going beautifully in the beginning, but I think we messed up when we allowed family members to introduce us to what I called generational patterns of debt. We ended up getting furniture from rental places, doing payday advances, high cable bills with premium channels, on top of a car note, car insurance, rent, utilities, gas, and food. We accumulated so much debt that we could have avoided if we didn't try to fill our apartment with fine furniture. We were 18 and 19 and didn't realize that we didn't need all of that right away. On top of that, the morning sickness that accompanied the pregnancy forced me to quit working. This was not regular morning sickness; it was aggressive and severe. I lost body weight but my feet swole so big that I couldn't wear shoes. I thought it was a normal part of pregnancy, so I didn't pay much attention to it, even though most of my days and nights were filled with feeling miserable. Jermaine was at work most of the time now, and I was at home alone and sick.

The vomiting would last all day, every day for the entire seven months of the pregnancy, and we didn't have a clue that a pregnancy complication was ravishing my body in the worst way and that my and my baby's lives were in serious jeopardy. Jermaine was working overtime trying to maintain all the bills and continue to take care of us. I can only imagine the stress that he was under, but he said he wasn't. He never complained. He picked up some side gigs and a shift at the *Post and Courier*, which was the local newspaper. I would go with him and try to help. The shift was from 2 AM to 6 AM. We were two tired people, but we did what we had to do. On one of his days off, we decided to visit his grandmother. Mrs. Brown was such a blessing to me. We'd watch the soaps, and girl-talk and laugh together. She let me take naps in her bed. There was always this white blanket on her bed that I'll never forget the feel of. Mrs. Brown was a MasterChef. Everything this woman cooked made you want to lick your fingers and bite your tongue trying to shove the food in your mouth. She was also a woman who walked with God and exuded the light of Christ throughout her life. I never heard her gossip or speak a bad word about anyone. She was a praying woman, and she showed me so much love.

This meant a lot since I was estranged from my maternal grandmother and didn't have a relationship with my paternal grandmother. That day I decided to visit my cousin, Andre. He was my Uncle David's son, David Jr's big brother. So, when I went to hang out with him, it was my Uncle David's house that I visited. They lived on the same street as Mrs. Brown, so I asked my love to drop me off while he went to see his grandmama. My Uncle David was usually at work or in his room when I came to visit. When I did see him, he would tell me the same stories of how he had seen me and my mom in the mall when I was little and he would tell my mother, "That's my brother's child. I know it is, you gotta bring her to the family!" My mother would confirm that growing up she knew both my uncle and his wife, who was Andre's mom, and that my aunt and her were pregnant with us at the same time. He was one of the many people who knew I existed. This would explain his warm embrace the day I met him. On this visit, he came out of his room and said, "Hey Niecey, let me talk to you for a minute. I don't know if you know what you're doing is wrong in the eyes of the Lord, but you aren't supposed to be committing fornication. Technically, you shouldn't be living together either, before marriage. Although the Bible doesn't say there's a law against living together, it does speak about not yielding to temptation, and not fulfilling the lust of the flesh. If you live with the person, the temptation to commit lusts of the flesh will maximize and become harder to resist." He went on to give scripture. He was sure to make sure I understood, and he let me know that sin leads to eternal separation from God and that God loved me and wanted me to spend eternity with him. The last thing he said was, "if he loves you, he will marry you and you won't have to pressure him to do it. Now that you have been made aware, you are accountable for the knowledge that you have been given." A hug, a kiss on the forehead, and an 'I love you, Niecey" was how he left me and went back to his room.

That information ate at me the whole ride home. When we got back to our apartment, I couldn't hold it. I told Jermaine what my uncle had told me. He listened and was quiet for a moment. When he answered, he said, "He's right. I know better and I know what we're doing is wrong in God's eyes." I told him that I wouldn't pressure him with marriage and that I would just have to go back to my grandparents until we decided to get married. Given the tragic events leading up to my leaving home, I really didn't want to go back, but I didn't want to live in sin either. He was extra quiet but after a few minutes, he said "Let's get married. I'll call my Granny." His Granny was his pastor. There it was, we mutually decided we wanted to get married. There was no down-on-one-knee proposal, no ring, no room full of people, no tears, no cameras flashing, no wedding, just two people 18 and 19 years old who decided that they loved each other and wanted to be married. To be honest, 20 years later, I don't regret the decision we made that day. I don't regret how we made the decision, or how we got married. Our marriage has lasted, and we grow increasingly happier and in love with each passing day. Don't let people make you feel like you need an extravagant, glamorous wedding. You spend money on the wedding for people who could care less if your marriage survives, and you won't see most of them again after they eat all your food at the reception.

Jermaine said when he called his Granny, she went under the anointing and spoke in tongues, and said, "This is of God, this is the Lord's will." We went to her church on a Friday night expecting to be married, but Granny had something else in mind. She wanted to make sure that we were equally yoked, so she allowed us to "tarry for the Holy Ghost" together. We both came through that night with the Holy Spirit, and she sent us on our way and told us to come back the next day. Of course, we had been living together and temptations rose when we got home but neither one of us gave in and I'm glad that we didn't. When we returned to her church the next day she asked, "Are y'all still saved?" I was so happy to be able to say yes, lol! On Saturday, August 30, 2003, we stood before the Lord, Jermaine's Granny-Pastor Carter, and two witnesses and became ONE. No fairytale wedding but we did have the happily-ever-after love. We lived together, saved as husband and wife, for one month before our baby girl made a surprise entrance into the world, and how early she arrived introduced us to a side of parenthood that we had never seen before.

Remember the swelling and the severe vomiting I mentioned? This continued for the entire seven months I was pregnant. I mentioned it to my doctor, and he assured me that everything was fine. During this time, the financial burden was becoming heavy, and we decided it would be best to let our apartment go and move in with a relative so we could save up some money as we tried to navigate through life. We had to do it without the help or guidance of anyone. My mother and I were back to speaking to each other, but she had done some shady stuff , so I was on the fence about her again. She had done us a favor by putting our car under her car insurance policy. Jermaine was paying for both his insurance and hers. We ended up getting a call from the owner of the car lot who financed the car. They stated that we needed to turn the car in because he was made aware that there was no insurance on the vehicle. I had no idea how he knew that. My mother came rushing over to our apartment. "Y'all gotta turn the car in," she said. In return I asked, "Why is the insurance not being paid? We pay you every month, I think you're spending the money he's giving you," I said. This woman looked at me and said, "And so what!" Every time I thought she couldn't go any lower, she did. I couldn't believe we were paying her the money, and she was spending it. This means we were riding around without insurance for who knows how long!! Then she replied, "Give me the keys, I'm gonna take the car back to the car dealer!" I got so angry and before I could think about it, I said, "No!!" Tomorrow the car will be out of your name. She left furious that another plan of hers didn't work! The next day we transferred the insurance to a friend and shortly after, we got our own.

"A Narcissistic Mother may perceive her daughter as a threat. When a mother criticizes and devours her daughter, she diminishes the threat to her own fragile self-esteem. As a daughter analyzes what her mother appears to be jealous about, she comes to feel unworthy." -Katie McBride Ph.D.

As life would go on, I realized that my mother was a narcissistic mother who never recovered from her own narcissistic mother. If you are experiencing this, I'm here to tell you that it can get better. Counseling may be a way of helping, but ultimately, deliverance would be the number one choice. God can heal a person from any and all sicknesses. In my opinion, narcissism is a sickness attached to the demonic spirit of jealousy. In order to get free, the mother would have to accept and admit that she is a narcissist, which could be hard. She may not think she's doing anything wrong. Pray and seek God for guidance, but if she shows no signs of change, take my advice! Set boundaries around the relationship.

Maybe you can't be around her for large amounts of time or maybe you must cut her off completely. Whatever you choose, remember to consider your peace, sanity, and self-worth first. Anybody who threatens to disrupt your peace or healing deserves to have their access to you denied. After this, we moved out and my health took a turn for the absolute worst. I wasn't getting much rest and one night I was sitting on the couch at Mrs. Brown's house. Jermaine had just ordered me some pizza when all of a sudden, my body began to hurt all over. Mainly, the pain was in my chest, the area under my right rib cage, my stomach, and my head. I started throwing up and I told him I thought I needed to go to the hospital. When he reached to grab his keys, he realized his dad had borrowed his car without him knowing. As soon as he came back, we hopped in the car and drove to the hospital. Everything was a blur after that. I remember having a headache so severe I didn't want to lift my head. The nurses checked my vitals. They said that my blood pressure had risen to stroke levels. My kidneys and liver were shutting down and they needed to deliver the baby ASAP, or it would be fatal for both of us. Jermaine called his Granny, who began to pray...

They gave me sedation medicine and a male nurse rubbed my forehead as I fell into a sleep, while they rolled my bed into the operating room. A C-section is what they performed and at 18 years old my body was undergoing a substantial amount of trauma, and my physical state now matched my emotional state. No matter how I tried to outrun trauma it would always find me, and it would make me pay. Pre-eclampsia is a potentially dangerous pregnancy complication characterized by high blood pressure. Although its exact cause is not known it's been said to occur when there's a problem with the placenta and stress. Pre-eclampsia may result in damage to vital organs, cause a stroke, and even fatality. The only cure for Pre-eclampsia is to deliver the baby and placenta. Our baby came early at 32 weeks. She was a gorgeous girl who weighed 3 pounds and 11 ounces. She had a tiny head full of black straight hair. She could fit into the palm of Jermaine's hand. She needed to stay in the Neonatal Intensive Care Unit of the hospital, hooked up to monitors and tubes until she could breathe and eat on her own. Having to leave the hospital without your baby is a painful feeling. It took an extreme toll on me. We traveled back and forth to the hospital to visit her. It was very cold out, and technically I was supposed to be at home while my body closed up.

The pain of the C-section had me down for a couple of weeks but after that, no one could keep me away from the hospital. My stepmother had volunteered to let us stay with them until we got on our feet. I was surprised, but we accepted the offer. Jermaine promised me he would have us in our own place in one month and I trusted and believed him. I don't think my stepmother did, though. I had heard that she had said to Jermaine at the hospital that the whole situation was his fault because I was stressed worrying about him and our current financial and living situation. I do believe the stresses of life contributed to my early labor, but it wasn't my husband's fault. For as long as I had known him, he'd always been hardworking. What we were experiencing was called life and had nothing to do with negligence on his part. We were young and trying to get our footing as young adults being on our own. I was angered that at a time like that, she would add the stress of making him feel like I was about to die because of him. I wanted to address it but decided not to, because we were living with her and my father for the time being. I felt like she overstepped her boundaries a lot when it came to me. She was nice at times, and sometimes she meant well, but other times she was condescending and passive-aggressive. She would take small digs that were just enough to sting me, but not enough to complain about because I would look foolish. She told me that my friends and I looked like hoes because we were wearing shirts with our bellies out. She mostly said things to me about my dad behind his back like how he felt about me during disagreements. These things always made me look at him differently. She had said many things that would hurt my feelings and help the wedge between my dad and me grow. My dad would say he knew she would say things that she shouldn't have said to me, but he was too weak to correct her.

He just let a lot of things slide. This woman started rumors, including one that mentioned that we only bought our first home because we got a grant, lol. Someone even told me she told personal information, which wasn't her place to tell, about my mother's health condition to another family member. As an adult, I achieved something major by starting my own business and she made a remark on social media, which was, "Well who would've thought!?" This one would have people calling me, asking me why she would say such a thing as if I was expected to be a failure. When I succeeded, there was a shift and a whole lot of, "I always knew you woulds." *Be careful with people becoming so "proud" of you all of a sudden because you turned into what they doubted you'd be from the beginning.* Still, we were grateful they allowed us to live there. Some said I didn't have anything to be grateful for though, since my father had done little to nothing for me to this point. I still was grateful because they didn't have to open their doors. Even though my dad was at home with his daughters (2 under 2), and I was there with my baby we still rarely spoke. He'd be in his room with his kids, and I'd be in the room we were borrowing with mine. Once we both walked out of our rooms at the same time, we smirked, nodded at each other, and continued to go about our individual tasks. Jermaine and Shanda would work all day and I was lonely. I was a young mom, recovering from a C-section and sickness with a brand-new baby. I was sleep-deprived and not really taking the best care of myself. My baby wouldn't nurse so she had to be formula-fed and I hated that. That meant getting up and down and making bottles! I'd go all day most days without eating because I didn't want to eat their food. I felt that was a good way to be considerate, as we weren't asked to pay any bills.

Jermaine would bring me food and we'd have our own snacks and drinks. Shortly after we moved in, the nitpicking started. One day Shanda came home from work and called me down to the kitchen. When I got there, there was a sink of dishes looking at me. She proceeded with an attitude to ask me, "You couldn't wash the dishes?" Now mind you, as long as I've known her(five years at the time) she always bragged about how when she had her babies, she never had to do anything right after, until she recovered. "Oh no, I just had a baby I'm not washing dishes; oh, I just had a baby, I'm not lifting anything heavy; oh, I just had a baby, I don't do this or Oh I don't do that!" So, we ignored the fact that I had just had a baby coupled with the fact that we rarely ate at their house. We even made sure to minimize using light and water! Honestly, I felt like *why am I being called down here with a baby on my shoulder to wash dishes, when you have a daughter of dishwashing age and a husband who was at home all day?* More than likely, they were the ones using the dishes anyway. I walked over to the sink to run some water. I was just going to wash them anyway. Shanda decided to grab my arm and I snapped. Up until this point, I had never been disrespectful, talked back, or even spoken up for myself. I said firmly "Don't touch me!" She was shocked and I ran up the stairs. I was tired of all the adults in my life! I never had a self-pity party though. I just kept believing that one day God was going to send replacements for all the adults who failed me in life.

I told Jermaine what happened, and he assured me that he had been putting money up so we could move. Then she started with the rule "Nobody can be in my house on Sundays while we're not here." They were members of what I heard someone say was a prosperity ministry, and neither I nor Jermaine were interested in going, so Jermaine's cousin Shannon was a tremendous help to us by letting him drop her off at work and keeping her car while she was there. I don't even know if she realized how much she helped us out at the time. So, because we couldn't stay in the house on Sundays unsupervised, he'd have to get up on his only day off, drop his cousin off, and we'd go sit at his grandmother's house. If the goal was to make us uncomfortable, she had succeeded. We persevered, and after one month my husband had all the money he needed to get us an apartment. We got our place in the same neighborhood as my dad's house. It was within walking distance. Shanda didn't believe us up until the day we moved out. She came over and flicked the light switch on just to see if we had lights. Again, overstepping her boundaries, but this time I was just so happy to have our own place. I ignored her with a smile.

CHAPTER 17

PUZZLE PIECES

We struggled for a bit in the area of transportation when we first moved into our place. Jermaine either caught the bus or a cab to and from work. The cab was $20 going and $20 coming back. We toughed it out until my Uncle B gave us a car. We were very thankful because even when he tried to offer Uncle B money for the car, he wouldn't take it. We now had a car that was paid off. It was a grey big-body Cadillac Brougham. We never forgot his act of kindness. Things were starting to look up for us. Jermaine had gotten the promotion from Assistant Manager to General Manager, which means he was head over his own store. He was on salary and received monthly bonuses. We were saved and living our lives for God, we joined my grandmother's ministry, The Anointed House of God, and Jermaine took his store to an all-time new level. He was rocking his position. Things were indeed getting better! We started to hang out with my cousin, David Jr, and some of the youth our age from the church. When Nala was five months old, we learned that I was pregnant again. I was nervous because of what had transpired in the last pregnancy but of course, my husband reassured me that we would be fine, and he'd take care of us. That pregnancy would be nothing like the last and he was right. I turned 19 years old, and my pregnancy was almost perfect. No complications at all and even more excited to find out that we were expecting a boy this time. Nala would have a little brother and the four of us would be a happy family. Jermaine Jr was expected to arrive in November 2004. Life was easier to maintain this time around. We opted out of the fancy furniture. We did get a TV and a family member gave us a sectional couch. We had a place to sleep. Nala had her bed and her playpen, and I kept the cradle she had for the new baby. We were content! My mom and I were back on speaking terms again. She adored Nala and was excited to be having a grand boy too. She called them Granny girl and Granny boy. He had a name ready before he was even born. To my surprise, my mother had gotten pregnant shortly after I did. It was crazy how we would both be expecting babies that fall. Unfortunately, my mother would miscarry her baby at home, and her friend who helped clean up the place would describe it as there was so much blood it looked like a crime scene.

I was sad for her because she was sad. I had been where she was. Losing a baby is a very painful feeling. I felt sad and depressed, and I couldn't quite understand why it happened. This is one of those things that some people never get over. I wondered what he or she would look like or what their personality would have been like. I'm hoping I'll get to see that baby one day when we get to eternity. Either way, I was all prepared to be there for my mom despite her behavior, but one day when we were conversing, she made an eerie comment that caused me to not even want to discuss the topic with her, ever again. Her comment was, "I guess God let my baby die so your baby could live." I wasn't sure if I knew what that even meant. I didn't know how or what to feel now. I wondered, *should I even let her around my children?* I'd leave it unaddressed until right before she passed away. Besides, what would come next would cause me to forget all about her comment for years to come. As my pregnancy progressed along, I tried to remain stress-free and calm, but there was something my mom had said years earlier when I had the incident with Henry that I'd been wanting to ask. I wasn't sure if she wanted to speak about it. One day when I was over for a visit, I decided to ask her. "Mama, do you remember when the incident happened with Henry, and you said I could tell you and you would believe me because it happened to you?" I asked. "Yeah Dani, I remember." "What were you talking about? What happened to you?" There was a short pause, and I could tell she was caught off guard and trying to gather her thoughts. She started to speak, and I wanted to say stop as soon as she started.

Dear reader, what I am about to explain has a bit of graphic details. Please be aware that what comes next may not be suitable for children.

"Dani, Granddaddy Charles is not my real father. He's my stepfather and from the age of 3 to 13 he molested me." I sat quiet and still for the entire duration of her speech. I felt the room that only she and I occupied become heavy. "It started in New York. My mother met him when she was pregnant with your Aunt Nikki. He would start by touching me when I was three and as I got older, he would put his finger inside my private area, and he told me if I saw blood to wash my panties out, he would taunt me, hide in the closet, and jump out at me. Then when he would go to the store, my mother would force me to go with him even though I told her I didn't want to go. As we walked, he held my hand and asked me if I remembered our "little secret" and remembered not to tell anyone. One day when we were out walking, he made me fall into the snow and my teeth began to bleed." *Oh my gosh, I wanted her to stop, but I didn't say a word!* "When I turned 13 years old my mother had left home, and he took that time to take advantage of me," she paused, and then continued. "He threw me on the bed, and… And he… Well, he raped me. He took his private part out and ejaculated on my pubic hair." We sat in a few moments of silence. Then she spoke again. "I got up enough courage to tell my mother. I sat on the bottom of her bed and said, "Mommy… Daddy molested me, and I told her the entire story. Do you know what she said to me? She said you lying B**** he didn't do anything to you. You can't even remember what happened to you yesterday, how do you remember what happened to you when you were three?? You are lying.!" I could only imagine the pain and anguish of hearing your mother spew out these words to you as you pour out how you've been violated by her husband. I thought I was going to be sick! She continued, "Everyone in the house turned their backs on me. They all would be in the room, laughing, and I wasn't allowed to come in. They called me names and told me I was ugly! My mother and sisters were very cruel to me. They shunned me badly in the house and I felt like such an outsider. When she did decide to take it to the police, I just wanted my mom to love me, but I was so damaged that I took it back and pretended like it never happened. I began to run away from home and at 16 years old I left for good. I used to be so worried that he would do it to you. One time when you were small and still wearing diapers, he was changing you and I thought he did something to you. I was trying to walk up behind him, and my mother came running and shouting "You don't have to watch him. He's not gonna do anything to her." Even after I moved out, I would come over just to look at you to see if I saw any signs. I used to be so mad to see you were just wearing a T-shirt and panties. I couldn't even bring myself to ask you if anything had happened to you." She stopped talking and all I could say was, "I'm so sorry this happened to you, Mama."

I felt so sorry and sympathetic for my mother. This explained so much. Right before my eyes, the missing pieces of a puzzle I had been trying to put together for the longest began to magnetically pull themselves into place and I could see a clear picture. It all made sense! My life rewinded in the spaces of my mind right there sitting at her bedside. I tried to focus on my mother's abuse, but my mind couldn't help to think that this man raped and molested her, and she made sure to take all of her other children with her, but she left me behind, unprotected, unaware, and uncared for, to be raised by her abusive violators.

She walked out the door one day and didn't look back…. and She left me….there.

To Be Continued….

ABOUT THE AUTHOR

anielle Singleton is a 39-year-old Wife, Mother, Entrepreneur, Author, Publisher, Mentor, Minister, Prophetess, and Intercessor. She is married to Emmanuel Singleton Sr and has been his wife for 20 years and counting and is the mother of their 8 beautiful children. Danielle loves God and has been able to minister to many through the word, gift of song, prophecy, and intercession. She owns and co-owns her Bakery and multiple other businesses with her husband.

Danielle has also been able to Mentor many women through her women's ministry FlourishingHER, and many girls and young women through her young women's ministry FlourishingHERtoo. Together she and her husband are the Founding Ministers of The One Flesh Marriage Ministry and a youth ministry, Chosen Generation. She hopes to continue helping and encouraging women and young girls to break free from the bonds of the enemy by sharing her testimony of how God took her from abandonment, rejection, abuse, and low self-worth, to being delivered, free, healed, and made whole! Aside from all things Ministry, Danielle loves to decorate, vacation where there's white sand and blue water with her husband, dance in her kitchen to Christian music with her children, and spend time with her friends and family.

Danielle became an Author/Publisher after the call to the assignment by God, which was prophesied over her life multiple times, by multiple men and women of God in over a 15–20-year span. *From A Broken Place* is Danielle Singleton's first published book.